The Map
Rediscovering Rock And Roll
(a journey)

The Map
Rediscovering Rock And Roll
(a journey)

by
Paul Williams

with a foreword by
Patrick Nielsen Hayden

and books
south bend, indiana

THE MAP, REDISCOVERING ROCK AND ROLL (a journey)

and books, 702 South Michigan, South Bend, Indiana 46618

Library of Congress Catalog Number: 87-7300
International Standard Book Number: 0-89708-166-8
    First Printing, 1988.
    Printed in the United States of America
    3 5 7 9 10 8 6 4 2 Pbk.
Library of Congress Cataloging in Publication Data

Williams, Paul
The Map, Rediscovering Rock and Roll
Includes index
    1. Music – United States – History –
    Miscellanea. I. Title.
[LB414.G11 1987] 351'.06'0164
ISBN 0-89708-166-8 Pbk.

Additional copies available:
                    the distributors
                    702 South Michigan
                    South Bend, IN 46618

for Bill Graham,
who has proved,
over and over again,
that you don't need a guitar
to be a rock and roll hero.

Acknowledgements

The author would like to thank Donna Nassar, Jan Simmons, Bobbie Brien, Ann Patty, David Hartwell, Kenta and Taiyo Williams, Howie Klein, Dennis McNally, Clyde Taylor, Bill Graham, Colleen Kennedy, Kate Hayes, Tom Yates, Larry Dekker, Dave Scheff, Steve Barton, Bob Darlington, Ed Stasium, Heather and Erik Ansell, Lory Colbert, Byron Hatcher, Steve Raymond, Patty Walsh, János Szebedinszky, Michael Goldberg, Joel Selvin, Phil Lesh, The Stone, Zohn Artman, and many others who helped and encouraged me on my journey.

Foreword

by Patrick Nielsen Hayden

This June I watched Paul Williams conduct a session on "Rock and Spirituality" (not his preferred title) at New York's Open Center, a Soho establishment devoted to those studies and pursuits usually lumped together under the rubric of the "New Age." Perhaps unfairly, I expected an Open Center audience to bring a particular set of preconceptions to this talk by the mightily spiritual author of *Das Energi*, and as I watched several pairs of eyes glaze over at the Violent Femmes and Bo Diddley records Paul played while the room filled up, I decided I wasn't far wrong. The evening proceeded from there to a lengthy conversational scramble about the virtuously idealistic 1960s versus the evil 1980s, including at least one appearance by the remark "what's the *matter* with kids today?", and ultimately wound up with much of the audience planted firmly in a state of what Paul was pleased to call "creative confusion." Paul's good at that. It's been observed by his friends that Paul can project the distinct impression that he's coming on to the world...really, though, it's okay; he respects our minds, and he'll keep making excellent conversation in the morning.

Generalizations are insidious (as, after promulgating some very good ones for pages at a stretch, Paul is quick to point out herein), but it seemed to me that a lot of people at the Open Center wanted to hear once again about the glories of the overtly Consciousness-Expanding (or, alternately, Politically Committed) rock music of a certain historic period now past, and perhaps to pick up a few good tips about where to find modern music that flies similar flags. Certainly they weren't prepared for a defense of the Top 40 as crucial to the creative zeitgeist of rock and roll, nor for excerpts from a brilliant essay[1] on the connection between voodoo religion and the music's historical roots, nor for digressions into the spiritual aspects of the aesthetic of hardcore, nor for enthusiastic diatribes in praise of (God wot) Prince. Spirituality, Paul seemed to be striving to remind them, isn't a genteel lifestyle accessory; rather, it's a matter of constant work, taking risks, exposing one's self to the dark and light alike. And, *mutatis mutandis*, so is rock and roll: thus, one of the central points in the book you hold in your hands.

Paul would say I have an Attitude about the sort of people who were present that night — Attitude being a term much bandied about in the present work. I won't deny it. Born in 1959 but raised in a family just hip enough that I had some idea of what was really happening in the world when I read Paul's first book on rock (*Outlaw Blues*) in 1970 when it came out, I've

---

1   "Hear That Long Snake Moan," by Michael Ventura, in his collection *Shadow Dancing in the U.S.* (Los Angeles: Tarcher, 1983).

never entirely escaped the feeling that the 1960s were a terrific party which shut down just about the time I arrived. My (g-g-)generation didn't come of age in a period during which the air was full of the sort of ambient money and resources which nourish the development of countercultures. On the other hand, no one of my age got shipped overseas to be turned into hamburger on exotically-named deltas, either, but my Attitude doesn't usually think of that. My Attitude is very touchy about tales of all the great stuff I missed, thank you very much. So when Paul suggested to his Open Center audience that in fact the greatest betrayal of the spirit of those times might be to put them in a box labeled "The Magical 1960s" (the spirit of those times having surely been very much Here and Now), and a woman in the audience stood up to respond that, nonetheless, there *was* something magic and ineffable about that era, and I failed to resist the urge to point out that most people remember their youths as magical no matter when those youths were, and she turned to me to demand "Well, were *you* there?", my face may have registered irritation but my Attitude was exultant: ah hah, I thought, just as I expected, pulling Age and Rank on me just like the old farts these people thought they were different from. So few experiences in life match the sheer pleasure of having one's prejudices confirmed.

The Map is not a book about having one's prejudices confirmed.

The Map is a book about the *experience* of rock and roll—as audience member, record buyer, transformed and ecstatic club dancer, participant in the creative circuit between performers and the performed-to. As an authentic and certified Historic Figure from Ancient Days (founder of *Crawdaddy!* in 1966, inventor of rock journalism, etc etc you can read the jacket bio) it would be hard for someone like Paul Williams to entirely avoid teasing us with tidbits of lore and reminiscence from long ago when the beat was made of iron and electric guitars were made of wood, but in fact that angle isn't what Paul's on about at all, having found himself in the (recent) time chronicled here once again seduced and overwhelmed by the immediate, palpable, and compelling Real Thing. The Golden Age of Rock and Roll — as any concert attendee or slam-dancer or headbanging metalloid knows at the moment of their greatest transport — is always Right Now.

The Map is a book which, while appreciatively examining all the ways that rock music taste has come to serve as a "universal language" within which we can announce to the world what kind of person we are, nonetheless works to avoid entrapment in all those little Attitudes that serve to block our appreciation of the world — and strives to tell the truth about what's actually happening out there in the territory. (*The Map* is a relief map, not a package-tour guidebook.) "Who shall we rebel against, now that we rule the world? I think we can and do rebel against our own self-images, the outmoded pictures we have, some left over from last week and others from ten or twenty years ago, that reduce our openness to new experiences and tie us down to boring, self-limiting patterns of behavior." Because *The Map* is in large part a memoir of Paul Williams's own journey of rediscovery, in its pages Paul himself can be seen wrestling between the attractions of the new and the established parameters of his self-concept as someone who likes this sort of thing, doesn't like that. At the beginning of Chapter Six there's a brief narrative of a browse through Tower Records which pinpoints perfectly all the guilty little unacknowledged debates we have with ourselves in such situations. Elsewhere, his reluctant seduction by Hüsker Dü's *Candy Apple Grey* ("Ugly shouldn't be this beautiful. This stop was not on my itinerary. I don't know what I'm doing here. Help!") serves as another good example of those experiences which we all have and usually allow ourselves to forget. (I, for instance, have always had my current impeccable tastes; haven't you?)

The Map isn't, primarily, about "Rock and Spirituality"; the title of that talk, remember, wasn't Paul's choice. "Spirituality," like "The Magical 1960s," is a box. On the other hand, *The Map* discusses at length — and with no implication that these are universal or even common perceptions — the role which rock and roll has consistently played in Paul's life, even during the long period when he wasn't paying attention to the new stuff and didn't feel he could write about the old without sounding like an Expert (which is to say remote, referential, detailed, and difficult). "Rock and roll touches me in places my mind is unaware of, afraid of, even places where my mind is forbidden to go. It is my shortcut to the unknowable inside me.... It has always functioned as a red-hot rocket ride out of comfort, familiarity, and security and into danger, passion, the unknown, creativity, and unreasonable, irrational joy."

And *The Map* is, very much, about that creative circuit between the stage and the dance floor, that space
in the midnight hour where, as the U2 song has it, "two
hearts beat as one": "the beat that gives rock its specialness...the moment of connection between musician
here and dancer here, something more powerful than
communication, something approaching simultaneous
awareness." Paul notes that his rock criticism in *Crawdaddy!* and *Outlaw Blues*, like most of the serious writing about the music since then, was primarily about
recorded music; with records, the possibility exists that
critic and reader can share the same experience. Much
of *The Map*, on the other hand, is about live shows,
from bars to arena events, and about the strange magics
peculiar to each sort. (For this reason alone one is
tempted to promote *The Map* as A Significant Addition
To The Critical Literature...but no, that's not it at all,
the critics can have their taxonomies and expertise
while *The Map* remains a book about rock and roll for
the rest of us. As Paul points out, the sense of Finally
Knowing How It's Done is the death of creativity, and
of true appreciation.)

The Map is about surprise, and delight, and the con-
struction and disassembly of models. It's also a marvel-
lously lucid and conversational piece of writing, without
a trace of the air of spurious authority which infects so
much serious writing on popular culture. The definitive
epigraph for the *Collected Writings of Paul Williams*
(Glen Ellen University Press, 42 vols., 2079) may be
found in the middle of a paragraph in Chapter Six:
"Perhaps this is obvious, but I find it quite striking." As
I've observed elsewhere, Paul's specialty is his ability to

redirect our attention to aspects of reality so obvious that we stopped noticing them years ago, and to hold that attention there long enough for us to grasp their real implications. In a significant sense *The Map* may be his best book yet, though don't hold me to it; I'll just say that a lot of people who've read it in manuscript during the last year are extremely happy to see it in print. More than anything else, though, *The Map* is about the energy of the moment, the primal zap at the center of consciousness that rock and roll aims for and, frequently, hits. "Playing in a rock and roll band is a great opportunity to get in touch with that energy," Paul remarks, but "another opportunity that's open to all of us is to be part of the audience. Either way, the experience is one of giving and receiving. You may never know — you the performer or you the audience — who you've touched or how deeply. It doesn't matter. The work of poetry, prophecy, and philosophy is to share the truth. The work of music is spiritual healing. The work of theater is to let us see ourselves. Put the three together and you have heavy magic indeed, something worth traveling from town to town for, whether there's money and success in it or not.

"The audience thinks, here comes another band. The band thinks, here comes another city. And then they meet in the night and dance."

Patrick Nielsen Hayden
New York City, August 1987

*"From immemorial times the inspiring effect
of the invisible sound that moves all hearts,
and draws them together, has mystified
humankind."*
— *The I Ching*
(Wilhelm/Baynes translation)

Introduction

We gotta start from the fact that it's overwhelming. I'm an idiot. That's how I feel when I look in almost any direction. I don't know anything about the current underground scene. I don't know anything about heavy metal. I don't know what's going on in black music. I don't recognize the names of most of last year's big hits. I never heard an R.E.M. record until today. I've missed almost every great concert and club appearance of the last fifteen years. And the list goes on.

Right away I think you're thinking, "How can this guy write about rock and roll if he hasn't heard — —?" Fill in the blank. And that's the thing. There are a near-infinite number of groups and songs and records to put in the blank. So I could be a guy who's listened to almost everything across the whole spectrum for a long time — in which case my experience of rock would be so different from yours or anyone else's we'd have no common ground. Or I could be a guy who's chosen a particular piece of the rock to identify with, who's real hip to what's going on there and rejects or ignores everything else. In which case you and I either understand each other perfectly or we don't talk at all.

Or I could be an idiot. Basically where I'm going here is I'm making a case that if there's to be a book that looks at rock music as a whole, that's in any sense going to explore and express the bigger picture, it has to be written by an idiot. Anybody who has to defend a self-image that they know what's going on is working with a tremendous handicap. The essence of what we're dealing with here is not facts or information. Past a certain point facts and knowledge are guaranteed to mislead us, because the essence of what we're dealing with here is mystery.

Rock and roll is not what we thought it was. It's lasted too long — well into its fourth decade now — and hasn't followed the path of anyone's expectations. "Rock and roll is here to stay" and "roll over, Beethoven" were heartfelt boasts, adolescent swagger, in rock's beginning years. Who would ever have imagined they might turn out to be true?

A friend recently pointed out an extraordinary thing: the phrase "rock and roll" has never gone out of style. It has meant different things to different people, has been a cliché practically since it was coined and has been ridden on and exploited by every imaginable person for every possible reason, and yet through it all "rock and roll" is always cool. People say, "I love rock and roll" like it's a core part of who they are, and it is. The words "pop music" don't begin to have anything like the same effect. Why? What is rock, and what does it stand for for people? As many deaths as it's died, overwhelmed with its own excessiveness, arrogance, pomposity, greed, becalmed as it has so often been in the seas of commercial acceptance, comfort, petty power plays, the distortions and ultimately the boredom of fame, why does it always find a new vitality, how does it manage constantly to return to life, as relevant and fiery as ever? What is this stuff?

To me rock is a living force, resilient and stubborn, outlasting all those who seek to control it, explain it, pigeonhole it, exploit it, own it or understand it. The only thing to do with rock and roll is participate in it. Dance, shout, turn on the radio, buy records, go to concerts, make music yourself, read about it, watch it on TV. Identify with your heroes, even when you know better. Destroy all myths and then watch yourself create new ones, acting from an impulse that is as old as humankind. Say what you're not, say what you are. Let it all out. Now.

What I seek to create for myself, and for you if you like the idea, is a map – not a linear map, that helps you get from here to there, but a representation, like a relief map, of the entire environment of rock and roll. I have no intention of organizing rock and reducing it to categories. I have no interest in writing out a chronological history. I'm not going to provide thumbnail portraits of the leading personalities. What I mean by a map is something small that represents, with an intuitive accuracy, something larger – something so large that it's hard to find your way around it without a sketch to tell you which highways connect to which others and where the restrooms are located.

And since this is not linear or chronological, and the subject matter has no beginning or end, the way to start is to jump into the middle of it. We could learn to love the fact that it's overwhelming. I'm saying let's go out tonight and immerse ourselves in the noise and bright lights and confusion of rock and roll. Find a patch of mystery, and dive on in.

Chapter One

"I hope we live to shout the tale..."

— Tears for Fears

L ate November 1985. I find myself on a most extraordinary adventure. It feels as though my life has been invaded — again — by rock and roll.

The first time this happened was twenty years ago. I can remember lying on my back on a hillside at dusk. I was releasing a tremendous charge of energy into the darkening sky. It was April; I was not yet seventeen. Earlier that day I'd purchased my first 45-rpm record since my sixth grade infatuation with Top 40 radio. The record was *The Last Time* by the Rolling Stones. I brought it home and played it, and played it again, and played it again, turned it over and listened to *Play with Fire* a few times and then played *Last Time* again. Finally I got on my bike with no plan or reason and pedaled for miles. I stopped by a field I'd never seen before. A sensation of great freedom came over me. I screamed at the sky, "this could be the last time!" Rage and frustration flooded out of me, and what I felt as I expressed them was sheer joy.

My days as a folk music purist were over. Six months later I was a rock and roll disc jockey on a college radio station, and a few months after that (January 1966) I started *Crawdaddy!*, "The Magazine of Rock 'n' Roll."

It was an experiment; I was an amateur; but the timing was right. I wrote a review of Simon & Garfunkel's *Sounds of Silence* album and Paul Simon called me at my college dormitory to say it was the first intelligent writing he'd seen about their music. I sent Bob Dylan the first two mimeographed issues of *Crawdaddy!* and he invited me to meet him backstage at a concert; a month later when I introduced myself to Al Kooper at a Blues Project show, he'd already heard about me and the magazine from Dylan. A producer friend played me the tapes for the first Doors album before it was released, and took me to hear them at a New York dance club. *Crawdaddy!* was the first national magazine to talk about the Doors, the Who, Jefferson Airplane, Cream, Jimi Hendrix, Buffalo Springfield, Janis Joplin, the Grateful Dead.

It was, of course, a fabulous time to be involved in the world of rock and roll. I edited the magazine from 1966 to 1968, and was still on the scene as a traveling journalist in 1969: I hung out at the first Crosby, Stills and Nash sessions, sang on John Lennon's *Give Peace a Chance,* and attended the Woodstock Festival. But the energy that had been rising steadily for four solid years finally peaked in 1969, and like a lot of people I found myself involved in other things in the 1970s. I still listened to rock music, still loved it, but it was no longer at the center of my life.

Now, 1985, thirty-seven years old, I'm sitting here surrounded by new records, music magazines, and scraps of paper with musicians' phone numbers and dates of upcoming concerts. In the past week I've been to six rock and roll shows. I've got an excuse: I'm writing a book. I'm being paid to do this. But I know that in fact I created the book project to satisfy my need to get back into the rock world again. What is it that's pulling me? And why now?

"I am coming home." The words jump out at me from the headphones as if in direct response to the question I just asked. The singer is Bono Hewson, 24 years old, one of four members of the Irish band U2. The record I'm listening to is a 1985 release called *Wide Awake in America*, an example of the interesting free zone that's been created in the 1980s between the traditional single (three minutes) and album (forty minutes). This is a "special low-priced collection of live recordings and out-takes" from the band's previous album. Side one is twelve minutes long and consists of two songs: *Bad (Live)* and *A Sort of Homecoming (Live)*. The two songs together are my favorite piece of music right now; I can listen to them over and over, a dozen times in a row, and still be excited, inspired, hypnotized. It's as though this is what I was looking for when I started listening to rock music actively (instead of passively) this past summer: music that would simultaneously open and express the deepest regions of my heart. Music that seems to be a part of the very moment I'm living in and listening in; music that is tough, honest, adventurous, ambiguous, uncompromising, and full of love. Music that will go on surprising me every time I let it in.

"Discovering" these two songs took some commitment on my part. People told me how good U2 were and I believed them (because I was looking for something good; before that you had to hit me over the head and tie me down to get me to really listen to anything new). I bought a U2 album and played it a number of times and felt good about it, bought another one and was impressed by that too, but still it was more like believing this music would really excite me if I listened long enough and at the right times. It hadn't happened yet.

Then I bought this one, mostly because it was on sale somewhere, and something clicked the first time I heard it — it had a sound that struck me right away. The next night I played the same side again, sitting and talking with my lover, and found myself playing it over and over, still not certain what it was I liked about it, but connecting more and more. "If I could, you know I would...let it go." It's like first you hear the truth in the voice, or the bass line, or the beat, and then you start listening to the words to try to find out what it is that's moving you so deeply.

The intent of this book is to tell the truth about rock and roll. This truth does not exist at a distance. U2 has another song called *Two Hearts Beat as One.* I suspect that the beat that gives rock its specialness is this beat, the moment of connection between musician here and dancer here, something more powerful than communication, something approaching simultaneous awareness. And everything else that falls under the umbrella of rock, even department stores selling

Madonna lingerie and politicians waving Springsteen flags, is an extension of that moment when performer and listener are one. I want to explore and express that moment, not least because I want to go on experiencing it. I know there's a risk that if you talk about the magic it'll go away, but there's a greater risk that if you don't talk about it it will shrivel up inside you and die.

Rock and roll is life-giving. When I wrote about rock in the 1960s something revolutionary was happening, and so what motivated me was to tell the truth about my own experience of the music in order to connect with and support others in my generation who were going through the same thing. Rock and roll expressed our feelings and thereby helped make things happen.

Now in the 1980s rock has shifted from being revolutionary to being a primary part of the cultural superstructure of our society. Some would say this means the revolution succeeded; others would say it means it failed. Both might be true. And there's a way of looking at it where we don't have to decide who won or lost; we can just see that it is what it is.

I'm not a partisan any more. I like rock and roll; but I no longer know if it will change the world. It has changed the world, no question about that; and it seems to have what it takes to go on changing as the world changes. But is it now an agent of change, to the extent that one promotes change simply by promoting rock and roll (as seemed true to me in the Sixties)? I don't know. Perhaps in the course of this journey I'll find out.

So I have this sort of messy agenda, as opposed to a nice, neat structure, partly because I like things a little messy, and partly because I don't believe a nice, neat structure will serve me in finding and sharing the truth about this music.

What's on the agenda? Certainly the politics of rock, from punk to Live Aid to senate hearings on rock lyrics. Then there's my search for the elements of rock and roll, those unchanging aspects of it that allow it to keep its identity, its edge, in the face of extraordinary wear and tear. What are they? And I have questions about who the audiences are, and whether they're as fragmented and divided as they seem to be or if there's some common ground.

What is rock and roll today, and what is it if we look at its entire thirty-plus years at once? I don't mean going through rock's history again. There are lots of books of rock history out, some of them very good; and you can get more rock history than most of us want just by turning on the radio or the TV any weekend or by reading the entertainment section of the newspaper. Every day is the twentieth or thirtieth anniversary of something.

The value of history is the perspective it gives us, the insight into ourselves and our institutions. I think more than anything what has drawn me back into the rock and roll world is a sense that if I can get an overview of rock, past and present, some important and exciting secret will be revealed to me.

¤

Three o'clock in the morning. Donna and I have just returned from San Francisco (an hour's drive), where we saw a truly inspiring show: the Kantner Balin Casady Band (three founding members of Jefferson Airplane, and four other superb musicians) at the original Fillmore Auditorium. The Fillmore along with the Avalon was one of dance halls where the San Francisco sound and much of modern American rock music were born, two decades ago. The Airplane was one of the leading bands, along with the Grateful Dead, of that fabulous era. But this was not a nostalgia show. The KBC Band is playing new music, music of the moment or maybe the future, and they are hot! It felt like being present at the beginning of something all over again. The audience knew it. They were walking out of the hall, down those famous old stairs, three feet off the ground.

The secret of the universe has to do with getting things in their proper place. The weight of history, all the things you've done and that people know you for, can be a burden or an inspiration. History had been a growing burden for the band called Jefferson Starship, and for Paul Kantner and Grace Slick, who'd formed the band in 1974 out of the ashes of Jefferson Airplane. Finally in 1984 the burden became unbearable; when the dust cleared, Kantner was free of the band he'd been holding onto and holding together since the Sixties and the other band members were free of their image of "tired dinosaur trying to stay hip." Everything shifted. In 1985 Starship (as they're now called) has a number one record, and history has moved to serve them: there's something exciting about a band that, instead of dying, streamlines and recreates itself and becomes more successful (by whatever standard; in this case size of audience and record sales) than it ever was before.

And history has moved to serve Kantner (and Balin and Casady, who also had the image of ex-Airplane hanging around their necks with every new project they

undertook in the last fifteen years) as well. The KBC
Band reopening the Fillmore with their hot new music
is a powerful image, affirming the past and opening a
door to the future. I personally am much more excited
about KBC than the Starship; but the point is that
sometimes when things get rearranged, everybody
benefits. The past can bury us, or it can give us a place
to stand and be seen as we reach energetically for what
comes next.

We are embarked on an adventure. I am starting to
realize and remember that this rock and roll journey is
not mine alone, but is in fact the journey of an entire
generation. "Don't you remember?" say the Starship in
their hit single, "We built this city on rock and roll!"
And while no two people might agree on exactly what
that phrase means, it has powerful resonances (positive
or negative) for almost everyone who hears it. How
could it not make number one? It's a feel-good flag-
waver, and the time was right.

There's a mystique to live rock and roll, and I've felt
it recently with KBC at the Fillmore, with the Grateful
Dead (true keepers of the flame, and a musical
phenomenon even more than a cultural one), with a
dynamic four-man band called Translator playing in
clubs around the Bay Area, and with the heavy metal
showmanship of Motley Crüe at what amounted to a
stadium-sized teenage party. There's a mystique to
recorded rock and roll, and I'm experiencing it this
month in LPs by R.E.M. (*Fables of the Reconstruction*)
and Talking Heads (*Little Creatures*), in the *Sun City*
anthology (a magnificently diverse gathering of
musicians, from Miles Davis to Afrika Bambaataa to
Ringo Starr, making a political statement that is also

powerful, creative music), in U2's EP *Wide Awake in America*, and in Tramaine's twelve-inch single *Fall Down* (the first gospel record to top the dance charts — "spirit of love fall down on me," oh yeah!). There's also a mystique surrounding broadcast rock and roll — embodied this month for example by Bruce Springsteen's *My Hometown*, which most rock listeners have heard dozens or hundreds of times as an album track, taking on new and different significance as a hit single on pop radio. The broadcast realm includes top 40 radio ("the hits"); all the other rock radio formats (soft rock, album rock); MTV and other rock video networks and programs; and the old standby of rock star appearances — two of the best-remembered collective events of the postwar era in the U.S., up there with JFK's death and the moonwalk, are the first appearances of Elvis (1956) and the Beatles (1964) on television's *Ed Sullivan Show*.

The pinnacle of the top 40 mystique is the number one record. This concept predates rock and roll — *Billboard* magazine launched its "Music Popularity Chart" in July, 1940, and that chart has continued to appear every week (it's now called "Hot 100 Singles") ever since. I'm personally convinced that rock music, even after the tremendous expansion in marketplace, form and creativity during the late Sixties, would not still be with us today except for the continuing existence of the top 40 and the hit single — in a strange way this most maligned, least self-consciously artistic sector of the rock and roll world is also the sine qua non, the one piece of the picture without which everything else would fall apart.

And rock and roll has an existence in another realm besides its basic forms of live performance, recorded music, broadcast music, broadcast video and (the next wave?) recorded video. For lack of another term, let's call this realm "the scene." The rock scene includes fashion or style; it includes all aspects of the star phenomenon; all talk about rock music, rock personalities, rock events, in books magazines newspapers, on radio and TV, around the dinner table and on the street; it includes the abstract quality of identification with a particular group or performer, and all the ramifications that identification has in an individual's life. It is pervasive. In our society, rock and roll is everywhere.

¤

Going to the Fillmore naturally brought back a lot of memories for me. The Kantner-Balin-Casady Band, when they were forced out for a third encore, did *Today,* a song I fell in love with the first time I visited the Fillmore Auditorium, in December of 1966, for a Jefferson Airplane show. The Junior Wells Blues Band was also on the bill, and at the Avalon Ballroom the same weekend I saw Country Joe and the Fish, and Moby Grape (Janis Joplin made a guest appearance). Strobe lights were flashing, liquid light shows were being projected on the walls, people were dancing in circles and painting each other's faces with fluorescent colors. The room was dark, sweaty, friendly, and full of marijuana smoke. The music was loud and its beat seemed to run through everything that was happening. It felt like a tribal gathering. I was eighteen. I'd never been to California before. I was impressed.

When I tell stories of some of the moments I witnessed and participated in in the rock scene of the late 1960s, people often respond with a tremendous wistfulness, expressing regret that they missed out on the magic of that era. If I were primarily a storyteller I'd probably relish that sort of response; it's an acknowledgment that my listener has been caught up in the projected wonder of a faraway place and time. But in fact it makes me uncomfortable. I don't like to talk about the untouchable, the unreachable, the unavailable. I prefer for my words to be an invitation, a seduction, a door to something you can create and participate in now.

So it's no accident that I find myself writing at a moment when there is again magic to be found in the world of rock music. Not that it ever went away — people have been finding it one place or another every day of every year since the first notes of *Rock Around the Clock* blasted out of the radio, and before that too — but there's a "rising tide" feeling about what's going on in rock now, and so much magic that can be reached in so many different ways that I don't feel like I'm leading you on when I share my own delight. I can even talk of great moments that are past and gone, confident that equally powerful experiences lie ahead for you and me and anyone else of any age who has the desire and the courage to jump in.

"INTERVIEWER: What do you think rock and roll will become? JOHN LENNON: Whatever we make it." (*Rolling Stone*, 1971) The surprising thing to me about my rock and roll journey so far, the adventure of the last few months, is that when I try to describe what I'm doing it sounds vague to me, sounds like I don't quite know—and yet when I look at the actions I'm taking, they seem energetic, purposeful, selective. It's as though there's an unconscious path of inquiry here that's very real to me, and I'm following it intuitively, deliberately, with a fierce, hungering sort of energy. Some part of me seems to know exactly what it's after, or anyway has very specific ideas about where to look.

I went to a Heart concert the other night, not because I'm a big fan of their music but because I felt I would learn something from being there. A lot of what I learn takes the form of questions, often rather obvious and simple-minded questions; in this case, it was, "Why do people come to these shows?" I'm here because I'm searching for the truth about rock and roll, but how about all the rest of you? And a crazy thought came to me: maybe they're here for the same reason.

It was at the Oakland Coliseum, a typical 1980s American sports/rock arena that holds 12,000–15,000 people (depending on how it's set up—in this case it was reserved seating, chairs on the stadium floor, whereas at a heavy metal or a Grateful Dead concert that floor is bare, so people can dance or jam up against each other or both). Heart has had two top ten hits in the last few months and I expected a mostly teenage crowd. I was wrong. It was a generic rock audience— i.e., not punk, not heavy metal, not art-rock; a combination working class and young professional crowd, no particular style of dress except casual—mostly between the ages of 20 and 30. On rethinking it, I realized Heart had been a very popular hard rock band in the latter part of the 1970s, and an identity band, which means lots of fans identified with them, particularly because the two most visible members of the band are women—

the lead singer *and* the lead guitarist. So my new guess is that this was a crowd of people many of whom had felt strongly about the band when they were teenagers, and who were coming out now to cheer their idols' comeback and get a little rock and roll recharge of their own.

I was surprised at how unresponsive the audience was. The opening act was Phantom, Rocker & Slick, a new group made up of two members of the Stray Cats (a defunct 1980s rockabilly group, superstars for a year) and a guitarist known for his work with David Bowie. Their first album is doing well and getting a lot of radio airplay, but the audience mostly ignored them or sat politely. This wasn't so surprising, because the group's performance was fairly insipid. The hot guitarist didn't seem so hot, the music was professional but mostly forgettable, and the frontmen's gestures and carrying on were quite inadequate for stadium rock. There was no real effort to win over the audience.

Heart came on after the obligatory 25-minute break (ostensibly set-up time, but it also serves as a chance for the crowd to socialize and buy more soda and t-shirts), and the contrast was so great that it occurred to me that the opening act's lackluster performance might actually be in their contract. The crowd was excited; no question about it. My sense of it is that they really loved Heart, and were very satisfied with their performance – energetic, professional, moderately flashy (Ann Wilson has a fine voice and good stage presence; her sister's nice to look at), likeable, unspectacular – right from the start.

What surprised me was that people stayed in their seats. I felt sure they'd stand up, at least the people sitting on the floor seats, as soon as the headliners came on, a phenomenon I've seen at most of the shows I've been to recently. But aside from one or two people here and there, the crowd stayed sitting. I kind of wanted to stand up myself, but given the general spirit of things, I was inhibited by knowing I'd only be blocking the view of the people behind me. Ann Wilson tried to get the audience to sing along a few times — she wasn't very inspired by the results, but she handled it like a trouper.

Then near the end of the show, Ann said, "here's something a little special for you," and Grace Slick and Stevie Nicks, two of the biggest female stars in contemporary rock (and both with big hits on the charts at the time of the concert), walked on stage. The crowd went wild — they actually stood up, clapping and whooping, and stayed standing through the next song, on which Grace and Stevie contributed some modest back-up vocals. Moreover, the crowd got excited enough to start filling up the aisles near the front of the stage, overwhelming the slight efforts of the security people to keep them in their assigned seats. This could have happened at any time during the concert, but it took the visiting superstar hat trick to raise the energy to that level.

It made me realize in a new way the power of the star concept. It wasn't as though either woman actually shared their talent with us — and anyway the Wilson sisters, also stars, had been doing that all evening without getting a whole lot of feedback for it. It was that they were there, all four of these famous women on stage together, and we were excited, dazzled, not by their presence so much as the idea of being in their presence.

I was excited too, and as people started to press forward I realized that something that had been missing for me at this show was human contact. I pushed myself into the crowd – it was fairly easy to get almost to the edge of the stage – and stayed there throughout the closing song and the encores. It made the show much more satisfying.

For the second encore, Heart came out with champagne glasses, and Ann announced they'd just gotten some *very* good news – their new album had made it to number one, the first number one record of their careers. It was another special moment, but the crowd didn't seem to know how to acknowledge it. They were already excited, they were already happy. I think they were already looking forward to going home and going to sleep, and telling their coworkers the next day what a great show they'd been to.

It felt to me like Heart would have liked to have really shared their excitement, their triumph, with their fans, and I think they could have done it in a club, or a small theater, even with the same audience (reduced in numbers to comply with the fire laws). But in that stadium, that particular evening, it was like bouncing a ball off a rug. It made me remember when I saw the Beatles in some Boston sports arena in 1966. They played for half an hour, and all I or anyone else could hear was screaming. It was exciting to be there. But the excitement had to do with stardom, not music. And if the Beatles had wanted to communicate with us, getting something going back and forth through their music in the moment, they wouldn't have had a prayer. No wonder they stopped being a live band after that summer. What's surprising is that they could stay together as long as they did after the joy of playing together was gone.

But I have to go on and say that the easy conclusion that what's wrong with rock and roll is that it's become stadium rock is false or anyway misleading. I'll be going to see the Grateful Dead at the Oakland Coliseum in a few weeks, and there's every possibility that they'll put on an excellent show, with plenty of energy going from stage to audience to stage and back again in a great feedback loop of creativity that couldn't exist without the responsiveness of the audience. They've learned to play the stadiums, and so have relatively young metal bands like Motley Crue, who regardless of musicianship created a show that just vibrated with energy in the Cow Palace a few weeks ago. It can be done. Indeed, I'm sure the Crue show was more exciting in the Cow Palace than it could have been in a smaller theater or club.

Some bands can make the stadium environment work for them. But that still doesn't mean that things could have been much different at the Heart concert if Heart had been better at what they do or had taken a different approach. Certain things are built into the context of the show. The Beatles in the summer of '66 were absolutely helpless, I think, to do anything but show up and let the audience scream. Motley Crue can make a show that is much more exciting than Heart's in a similar-sized stadium because they're playing a different kind of music—and the difference is above all one of context. I'll go into this more later, because it offers a clue to what heavy metal is, and (I'm beginning to suspect) why it's such a vital part of the contemporary rock and roll scene. It's a wonderful mystery, because

Heart and Motley Crüe could be playing some of the same songs, and certainly do play the same instruments and achieve a sound that might be quite similar if the volume levels were the same. But context changes everything.

This is fun. I like being an idiot in such a huge and complicated playground. I like being a blind man methodically, intuitively, maybe randomly swarming all over this elephant, aware of but not necessarily moved by the pronouncements of all the other blind experts standing around. I appreciate that rock and roll is still here to be discovered, and I promise you I won't finish the job. Rock and roll and its implications are big enough that there'll still be plenty of mystery left when you and I have finished this adventure together and explored as much as we feel like exploring. The hard part for me, and probably for anybody, is to stay an idiot. As long as you do that, in any field of knowledge, you can always go back for more.

Chapter Two

"A million faces at my feet/but all I see are dark eyes."
— Bob Dylan

Self-image is important. I was thinking today that one of the reasons I became a volunteer fireman was it fit the person I liked to imagine myself being. Another, and separate, consideration, was how it might look to other people. That's called public image. And there were other factors in my becoming a volunteer that had nothing to do with image: for example, the excitement of it, the comradeship, the satisfaction of being of service. But self-image — "I'm a responsible, courageous, involved person; I'm a regular guy, part of the community" — definitely played a big part.

I bring this up because self-image and public image are big factors in just about every aspect of rock and roll. When I was a kid I was a Stones fan, not a Beatles fan. I liked the Beatles, but, you know, I didn't like the Beatles the way Beatles fans liked them. I liked the Beatles when they were tough — *Daytripper, Ticket to*

Ride, I'm Down — but it wouldn't have fit my self-image for me to *love* a group that anybody and everybody could love. Beatles songs tended to bore me after a while. The Stones, on the other hand, I could listen to forever. It was a big crisis for me the day I stopped sneering at the Beach Boys and let them into my heart. The truth was I'd long been impressed by *Shut Down* and *I Get Around*, but that didn't change the fact that their clothes, their haircuts, their lyrics, their crooning harmonies added up to putrified essence of everything I'd always known was uncool. But their music won me over in spite of myself, and so I mollified (and modified) my self-image by reading Derek Taylor's article in *Hit Parader* about Brian Wilson the genius and his breakthrough album *Pet Sounds*. I hitchhiked across the eastern United States in the summer of '66 listening to *God Only Knows* on a portable radio and seeing myself as this cool guy who had the guts and the good taste to appreciate the Beach Boys' genius even though everyone I knew sneered at them.

Self-image as much as public image (along with a genuine desire to help and a thrill at the power of it all) motivated the individual rock star participants in 1985's unprecedented fundraisers, *We Are the World*, Live Aid, Farm Aid, *Sun City*. This is significant because as you become a star, particularly a superstar, you tend to lose your personal freedom. The people around you (managers, press agents, record companies, friends, dependents) participate in more and more of your decisions. A natural outgrowth of this (and of being so public) is that public image becomes more of a motivation than self-image. So when rock stars decide to be

part of something because it's important to how they
see themselves (rather than how someone says the
public will perceive them), it's unusual, it means something, and the event that results tends to have a lot
more life in it, and a lot more impact.

Self-image as a motivation is essentially sincere;
public image usually is not. One arises from a genuine
personal need; the other comes from the mind, the in-
tellect, and tends to be manipulative.

This distinction between self-image and public image
is often blurred, for a simple reason: it is human nature
to be influenced by the values and interests of those
around us. So a human being tends to want to see himself as one who is into what the peers he most admires
are into, or as one who isn't into what the peers he dis-
dains are into, or as one who is noticeably cutting out a
different path from what seems to be the common
direction. He acts in reaction to others, and so it's easy
to assume, looking from outside, that his motivation is
to make an impression on others. In other words, it
looks like this teenager likes Iron Maiden or Wham!
because he or she wants to make a good impression on
his or her peers. Conformity, motivated by concern for
public image.

But most of the time public image (these are the
clothes I have to wear, this is the music I have to listen
to in order to be accepted) is only a secondary motivation. The teenager, or whoever, looks like he's primarily motivated by how he appears to others, but in fact his
primary motivation is usually how he appears to himself. "I'm the kind of guy who likes Iron Maiden; I'm
not one of these wimps who just listens to the latest top
40 theme-from-the-movie garbage." This distinction is

important because it means that people's choice of music goes deeper than just keeping up with the trends for social purposes; it (especially in adolescence) becomes deeply connected to one's sense of personal identity. This makes for a much more passionate and long-lasting connection than social considerations ever could.

Self-image has to do with identity; public image has to do with appearances.

My lady Donna, who's reading over my shoulder, asks an interesting question: Why now? Why did *We Are the World* and "Live Aid" happen this past year, rather than some other time? Why does it feel like there's some kind of social and personal awakening taking place in the music now? If what has motivated most of the rock and roll participants is self-image, a need to see themselves as part of something meaningful, why has this come to a head now rather than at some other time? And will it keep going?

My answer is, I don't know. I'm pretty sure the participants don't know either. You can trace a certain amount of cause and effect, Bob Geldof organizing Band-Aid because of a Peter Gabriel song and a BBC-TV documentary, American rock stars organizing something because the success of the British record caught their imagination, and so forth. You can say the timing of the African famine itself determined it, or that the heavy western TV coverage of the famine for a few months in 1984 was a major factor.

But there has been great need before, without any noticeable response from the rock community; and there has even been superstar response before (The

Concert for Bangla-Desh, 1971) without much ongoing impact.

Cause and effect is only part of the story. It's an interesting part, certainly. Why did it suddenly become vital to the self-image of many rock superstars (and less visible people working with or at least not against them) to channel energy and money and attention to the needy in Ethiopia or the worthy in the South African struggle? The evidence is, when we look closely, that the commitment and example of a very few people, at the right moment, was enough to set a lot of powerful people and events in motion. One person can definitely make a difference.

The rest of the story has to do with timing. Something is happening in music, something is happening in the world. It isn't even necessarily a good thing; just a motion, a flurry of activity. Why now? Why the Beatles in '64, Jimi Hendrix the Doors *Sgt. Pepper* the San Francisco Sound in '67, Woodstock (and Altamont) in '69? I don't know. But I enjoy thinking about the question, and my purpose in this book is to provide you with tools that may prove helpful as you search for answers of your own. And also to call you out to play, if you're not doing so already, because I do think we've entered another very special, very exciting era in this playground called rock and roll.

Headline in the Jan. 6, 1986 *San Francisco Chronicle*: "State Task Force Blasts Punk Rockers." The story below tells us that the governor's task force on youth gang violence "found that punk rockers belong together with followers of heavy metal and satanism as a new type of criminal gang that preaches 'anarchy' and 'bizarre violence and sex.' " (That's as opposed to the normal violence and sex that the governor's men go home and watch on tv after a hard day of task-forcing.)

The single most important issue regarding image and rock and roll is the way we use this music to tell ourselves who we are (and by extension and not as important, the way others use our choice of music to identify who they think we are, as in the headline above).

Don Henley's lovely hit single *The Boys of Summer* has a line about seeing "a Deadhead sticker on a Cadillac." That's a nice bit of Americana and a sort of obvious irony about how the times change (a Deadhead is a Grateful Dead fan, and by extension, at least in the public perception, an unreconstructed hippie). There's a neat twist in it about self-image, too, in the sense that the person owns the Cadillac in order to say something to himself about who he is, and then adds the Deadhead sticker to refine that statement: "I'm a success in this world, and I'm still a crazy fool for rock and roll."

It is clearly important to the self-image of millions and millions of Americans who are now in their thirties and forties to see themselves as still crazy about rock and roll. Many of us harbor secret or not-so-secret fears that we're losing touch with rock, we don't know what's going on, maybe we don't really like loud music any more...we're growing old. So our connection with rock becomes, among other things, a way of telling ourselves we've still got our youthful passion, we're not ready to be put out to pasture yet.

This in turn creates a problem for our children. How do they establish the separateness from the adult world that we once established by identifying with the Rolling Stones, if their parents are Rolling Stones fans? Punk and heavy metal both serve this need, in different but related ways, by being loud and violent and offensive enough to drive away or disgust or piss off all but the weirdest or wimpiest parent figures. It should be noted that teen heart-throbs like Duran Duran and Wham! can also fill a similar role: they make Daddy and Mommy throw up.

I'm falling in love with a group called Translator. "Love" seems like a strong word but it's the only way to describe how people feel about the bands or performers they're drawn to: people love Bruce Springsteen, they love the Grateful Dead, they love Rush, Yes, Led Zeppelin. This definitely goes beyond self-image. Self-image opens the door, and then the group's music, their art, draws you in. If it's really for you, it just draws you in further and further, a neverending voyage of discovery, power, delight.

Translator is four guys: a drummer, a bass-player, and two guitarists who also do the singing and write the songs. They have the gestalt quality of a mid-60s group: four striking and quite distinct personalities who add together to make something with a character of its own, different from and more than the sum of the parts. They've been playing for six years with no changes in personnel, and in fact have spent close to every day together during that time. Their age range is 31-33.

Translator has made three albums, none of which has sold many copies. 1985 was a particularly rough year: they recorded a third album with excellent material, then went to India and shot a video to promote the song their record company picked as a single, but neither the video nor the album received any significant airplay. They were excited about going on a national tour to promote the album and to show the rest of the country (they're a California band) how great they are live, but tours fell through and got delayed. Finally they got a chance to tour as an opening act for the Kinks, afte which they'd go on and do shows of their own in Nev York and New England; but after what seemed to them two great shows the Kinks fired them from the tour, and as a result their own shows also had to be cancelled, even though they were sold out, because without the Kinks tour there wasn't enough money to get them and their equipment to the east coast. But never say die. They scheduled a run of Bay Area gigs to pay the bills and made plans to go back in the studio and record a fourth album.

My introduction to the group began when Howie Klein gave me a copy of their third album. Howie is a guy I knew back in 1967 in New York, when he was a college student putting on rock shows (he booked most of the great west coast groups of that era for their first east coast concerts), and I was a college dropout editing a rock magazine. I saw his face on the cover of a local rock paper a few years ago and learned that he had become a central figure in the San Francisco punk/new wave scene (as a disc jockey, writer, club manager, wheeler-dealer) and was now president of a local new wave record label (415 Records) distributed by industry giant CBS. In the summer of '85, as I found myself consumed with curiosity about what had become of rock and roll, I thought of Howie and we got together again after not seeing each other for 17 or 18 years.

So I'm sitting there with Tripsmaster Klein, as we used to call him in the old days, hearing horror stories about music business '85, and he played me some tracks from a new 415 album just being released by a group

called Wire Train. I tried to explain what this rock and
roll book I wanted to write would be about, and as I left
he gave me a copy of Wire Train's album and of the
Translator album that had come out a few months earlier.

I'd had this idea in my head (I don't know about you,
but I almost always have ideas in my head before I hear
any new group, and they're almost always wrong) that
anything released by a new wave record company in San
Francisco in 1985 would be some kind of noisy frantic
angry experimental punk-related sound. Wire Train
surprised me by being melodic and Dylan-influenced, a
sophisticated modern sound but still more related to
some of my favorite Sixties music than to what I imagined was happening in the Eighties. I liked the band
a lot, and could easily see myself (self-image) becoming
a fan of theirs. I played the Translator album and that
also was very different from what I'd expected — upbeat
and open rather than dark and menacing. It seemed
more of a pop sound than Wire Train (didn't fit my
image of myself as a guy who likes what's daring and experimental). But I taped both albums and played them
in the car, and while I still like Wire Train, it was
Translator that came from behind and got me totally
hooked.

I've been wanting to tell the story of how this current
rock and roll journey of mine began, and I think the
time has come. I was on a vacation trip in Oregon with
my two sons (ages 10 and 12), and they convinced me to
buy two tapes — Sting's solo album and Springsteen's
Born in the USA. Both tapes were a lot better than I'd
expected — I'd been a big fan of Springsteen's in his
early days on the scene, 1973-75, saw him literally

dozens of times around New Jersey and New York, but he never touched me on record the way he always did in person, and after trying unsuccessfully to like *The River* I just let him go, as I'd let go the Stones and Lou Reed and Neil Young and the Beach Boys and God knows how many other old favorites. You buy somebody's record because they never let you down, and then you find you're just not listening to it, and you don't know if it's you that's changed or them, and you buy the next album and the same thing happens and after a while you just have to let it pass.

And then you find — anyway, I found — that most of the records you buy are records you've bought before, oldies from ten or fifteen years ago that you want to hear again, or maybe you want a copy on tape to listen to in the car. Maybe there's someone from the old days you're still loyal to — for me it's been Bob Dylan, although I know lots of Dylan fans who've stopped listening to his new stuff (wrongly, I think). And maybe there's an occasional new act that you get interested in or turned on to — I got excited about Prince with the *Dirty Mind* album, I got into the Pretenders after hearing *Middle of the Road* on the radio and bought their old lps as well as their new one. But all in all my image of myself as a rocker, a person in touch with the music and what's happening, was in shreds. People would ask me what new music I was into, and I'd mention Tom Verlaine, and then I'd have nothing else to say. (It was worse, however, when Verlaine was still in the band Television — I'd tell people I liked Television and they'd say, like admitting a guilty secret, that they were really getting into watching TV lately too.)

I'd heard that Bruce's new album was good, and I'd even seen the *Dancing in the Dark* video at a friend's house and loved it, but a year had passed and I still hadn't gotten around to buying the record. Quite a contrast from the days when I converted everyone I knew to Springsteen fans and got them to drive me to concerts a hundred miles away!

So we listened to Sting and Springsteen as we drove through Oregon. And we also listened to Bob Dylan's hot new record, *Empire Burlesque,* and we listened to Prince's *Around the World in a Day* and Madonna's *Like A Virgin* (also purchased at the boys' request), and we listened to *Songs from the Big Chair* by Tears for Fears. Springsteen and Sting marked the turning point for me, somehow I couldn't pretend any longer that all these good albums were just exceptions to the generally dismal state of rock and pop, but it was Tears for Fears that set me up for the revelation, Tears for Fears and their single *Shout* that made me ready to believe that rock and roll could once again be a major source of joy and awakening in my life.

Rock music is everywhere in the 1980s. I first heard *Shout* walking past a record store in a mall. I didn't like it, but I was struck by it — it seemed clever, and the phrase "these are the things I can do without" stuck in my mind. Then my kids mentioned that my ex-wife was promising to get the Tears for Fears album because she'd been completely captivated by their earlier hit *Everybody Wants to Rule the World.* I heard parts of *Shout* a few more times in public places (notably the local grocery store, which often has a rock radio station playing), and one day I noticed to my surprise that I was waiting to hear it, wanting to hear it.

I didn't know who Tears for Fears were, but I had some image of them in my mind anyway, just based on the name or their faces on the album cover in the record store window. I imagined they were some slick, popular, teen-oriented British group like A Flock of Seagulls – about whom I knew and know absolutely nothing, except that I'd seen a disparaging mention of them in a music magazine, as an example of what's wrong with modern rock/pop. And "Tears for Fears" sounded to me like the same kind of name as "A Flock of Seagulls" or "Men at Work." It's amazing how quick we are – speaking for myself, but I think it's true of many of us – to form opinions, especially negative opinions, based on just about nothing.

And what broke through those baseless but stubborn images in my head, images of what a popular group called Tears for Fears must be about and why I wouldn't like them, was exposure to a particular song that really connected for me. Exposure – not hearing the song once, but hearing it or parts of it over and over in a fairly short period until I'd learned its language (each song has its own language) and it started to speak to me. Actually it was speaking to me the first time I heard it, but I didn't recognize that or want to admit it. Exposure brought me to the point where I was letting it in, feeling it and knowing I was feeling it and loving every moment of it. Barriers dissolved. Communication happened. I personalized the song, made it be about my own situation and feelings.

So driving along with *Shout* on the tape player uniting me with my sons and with the world (the song had been number one all over Europe months before it was even released in the United States), listening to Bob

Dylan scream "When the Night Comes Falling from the Sky" as if to announce that passion has entered our lives again, I was primed for the (belated) discovery that Bruce Springsteen had made as close to a perfect car stereo album as anyone could hope for. My heart was even open enough to find pleasure in Sting's brilliantly-realized jazz-rock constructions (though his pretentiousness wore on me pretty quickly). And I guess I started to wonder, if there was all this happening right here in my car, what else would I discover if I started opening myself again to contemporary rock and pop?

I came home and listened to *Shout* with Donna under the influence of a mild psychedelic (drugs and music, just like the old days), and the next morning I found myself wanting to write about rock and roll. Those old voodoo rhythms had got me under their spell. Again.

So I bought more records, and visited Howie Klein, and went to New York to get myself a book contract, and when I came back I saw that Translator was playing at a club over in Cotati. I caught their act and liked them and decided one of the things I'd like to find out is what it's like to be a band trying to survive and make good music and get the world's attention in the mid-1980s.

It's a few months later, and I've been with Translator as they suffered intense paranoia about what the record company might try to force them to do and deep soul-searching about what it was they wanted to accomplish if they could possibly do it their way. And I've hung out with them in the studio as they and their producer Ed Stasium recorded an album that's much, much better than the previous one (and I liked the previous one).

Next comes the mixdown, and the effort to sell the product (which is different than what Translator thinks CBS thinks Translator should be) to the company, who in turn might sell it (with the band's help) to the world. It's funny. I feel like I connected with this band almost randomly, although I'll give myself credit for recognizing something good when I hear it. And I remember how this process happened for me before, like when I heard the Doors' tape, or when I heard an obscure single one night on one of the few radio stations ever to play it, became haunted by it and tracked down a copy, then made a point of looking up the band when I visited Los Angeles — the song was *Nowadays Clancy Can't Even Sing* by Buffalo Springfield, an early Neil Young ditty, and when I heard them at the Whisky in L.A. they had just that week recorded *For What It's Worth*. So it wasn't like I was listening to demos by every new group that came along and I decided this would be a great one. I just stumbled onto them. I got lucky.

When I listen to the tracks Translator has laid down in the last few weeks, I feel like I got lucky again. But we'll see how it goes in the mixdown sessions. (If it's really great music, is it possible for it to get lost in the mixing process? Good question.) And we'll see if the world agrees.

(Sometimes the world takes a long time to come around. It took ten years or more before the Velvet Underground had the reputation I thought they deserved in 1968. But then in 1968 I felt foolish because my friends had been telling me how great the Velvets were since early '67, and I wouldn't listen.)

Self-image, the way we see or want to see ourselves, plays a big part in the formation of attitudes. Attitudes dominate the rock and roll landscape. Elvis's sneer was an attitude. Punk rock and heavy metal are attitudes as much as they're musical forms. Critics' attitudes as conveyed through newspapers and magazines can have a tremendous impact on our receptiveness to certain records, performers, or whole categories of music, even though we believe we don't listen to critics. Fashion is an attitude. And particular attitudes go in and out of fashion, although that sneer does seem to show up in practically every era and every incarnation of rock and roll.

Like most things, attitudes play both constructive and destructive roles; attitudes make much of the greatness of rock music possible, and attitudes also tend to be the biggest obstacles to you and me as individuals enjoying the wealth of good music that's available to us. Call a record "hip hop" and rock intellectuals will approach it like it has a shot at authenticity, even greatness; call the same record "disco" and most of them won't touch it with a ten-foot pole.

If there is a revolution taking place now, it is a listeners' revolution more than a musicians' one (although the musicians may reap great benefits); and it is certainly a revolution of attitudes.

A larger and larger percentage of the people of the world, and of the decision-makers in our world, are people who've grown up listening to rock and roll. Too much can be made of this fact, and often is; but it is true that the influence of rock and of rock attitudes is growing year by year. It is also changing, taking new forms; some of these forms arrive with extraordinary suddenness and impact. Some are less important than they seem at the time; others are more important; but they all stir things up.

And there's a feedback effect; as the music touches more and more aspects of contemporary life and culture, the music itself changes, grows more confident here or more self-conscious there, intoxicated by its newfound power or scared of it or sometimes both at once. One of the things that is growing and changing unpredictably now is rock and roll's attitude towards itself. Who shall we rebel against, now that we rule the world?

I think we can and do rebel against our own self-images, the outmoded pictures we have, some left over from last week and others from ten or twenty years ago, that reduce our openness to new experiences and tie us down to boring, self-limiting patterns of behavior. This is an ongoing process, and an exciting one. We have to keep challenging our own assumptions, and to do that we have to notice our assumptions, recognize our attitudes as attitudes, not so we can live without attitudes (impossible) but so we have the freedom to break through them or push them aside when they get in the way of something more important.

Rock and roll is more than thirty years old. I'm sure I thought it would be dead by now, and it seems to me that for many years I acted as if it were dead. Maybe that's because there was nothing happening, or maybe I just didn't have ears to hear. Doesn't matter. What I like about this music is there's no entrance requirements: anybody, anytime, can get into or get back into the game.

The enemy of the "Live Aid" spirit (says me) is taking Live Aid too seriously. The secret of rock and roll is spontaneity. And it's a funny thing about spontaneity (to paraphrase T-Bone Burnett): as soon as you figure out how to do spontaneity, you're no longer spontaneous. And right at that moment some snot-nosed kid will come along and do it his way, making all the mistakes that you know better than, and inexplicably (probably because of payola or the sheer stupidity of the audience) get them all moving over to his tent.

And if it doesn't fit your self-image to sneak over and have a look at what's happening in that tent, that's fine. But you just might be missing something.

Chapter Three

"Maybe these maps and legends/been misunderstood."
— R.E.M.

So let's get serious. It's 1986. I'm sitting in front of my word processor, the letters fly up silently onto the screen, and over against the wall is this little portable compact disc player and a scatter of discs. I don't think we're in Kansas any more, Toto. This is the new age.

The rock groups I listened to were always a few years older than me. Now they're younger. What happened?

When I jumped on the scene twenty years ago, a snot-nosed kid, the territory was wide open. Nobody could even imagine what it would mean to write "seriously" about rock and roll. Today, well, today...

Today I open this big glossy magazine called *Spin*, and here's Pete Townshend leaping high in the air with his guitar and his grimace, and all around him the good old Townshend interview, latest edition, and listen to what he's going on about:

"...at the moment literature is connected with a certain strain of rock writing, which is something we're quite comfortable with now — this is assuming that one accepts rock writing as a legitimate form. In fact, it's more than a form. It's a complete environment, comparable to the Western, that enables you to relive formative experiences. There's a kind of mythic quality to much rock writing. It alludes to this thin air bubble floating in the sky known as MTV. You can speak a language there where nothing you say needs to make sense, but everyone understands you anyway."

You could poke fun at that, I suppose, but actually it's brilliant. He's right. I got nothing whatever to add to that. And on the facing page there's this multicolor ad from Sony, only $29.95, "a world premiere on home video," *John Lennon Live in New York City, 1972, never before seen, "Come Together own this treasure." I kid you not. I'm not being ironic. This is just what is.*

So what can a poor boy do, eh? Sit back and take it all in, I guess. And this current crop of critics/writers/-whatever is as hip as anyone could ask, I'm not being ironic, that's how I found out about R.E.M. and U2 and Los Lobos and the Replacements and more good stuff where this came from. It's a golden age out there. Rock and roll has never been healthier. And what right I have to be cadging free concert tickets off of this smoothly-running machine is something I can't figure at all. Everything's been said and if it hasn't it will be, and quite well too a lot of the time, reluctant though I am to admit it. You lot don't need me.

¤

But Donna really stuck it to me. She says, "so why don't you just tell your editor you made a mistake, accept the embarrassment, cancel the contract, add another debt to your collection? What's the worst that could happen?" And I say, "the worst that could happen is she'll laugh in my face, and tell me to go home and get to work."

So my five-year-old stepson had this question for his mother (he was listening to Prince sing *When Doves Cry* on the car radio): "What if every radio and TV and everybody in their house were playing this song at the same time, all over the world?" Here is a kid who understands rock and roll. Tramaine's extraordinary, ecstatic *Fall Down* flirts with a similar apocalyptic vision: "In my heart, in my soul, in my mind – all over me" (apocalyptic and intimate at the same time) "...must be the moment I heard Him say would come." And while she's screaming "spirit of love, fall down on me" (hit me with your best shot, Lord), she also manages to comment on what's happening in the collective consciousness – "hearts of stone are changing all around me..." In other words, if I understand rightly, there's this movement on the street; seemingly incorrigible dudes and chicks are being touched and changed by the holy spirit. This to me is a classic characteristic of rock and roll: it reports the news, the real news, talking about the moment as if it mattered, as if it wasn't just the same as every moment that ever was or will be. This is passion. This is a way for the collective mind and heart to send a message to itself.

Tramaine's song has an unbelievable rhythm track, and it still rocks during the 67 seconds of a cappella singing at the end of the twelve-inch version. The groove is so strong (and her voice so riveting) that even the silent implication of rhythm can drive right through you.

Another hot track from a whole different culture (Tramaine is an Oakland gospel singer, old pro, working with a state-of-the-art studio whiz, Robert Wright; this other is garage band culture and sound, a Minneapolis group known for '70s covers and drunken unpredictability) is *Hold My Life,* the lead song on the Replacements' *Tim* album. "Hold my life/until I'm/ready to use it," sings Paul Westerberg, putting just the right slurred emphasis on each syllable; "hold my life/because I just might lose it." I've listened to this thirty times in a row, and it still sounds good (better and better, in fact; raw elegance, every tossed-off note and hoarse vocal precisely in place, thousands of rough edges shining like so many diamonds), and still dances just out of reach of my mental grasp, in terms of being able to say "this is what he's talking about." It's not trivial. If rock and roll were a single person, this would be him after having accepted, explored, mastered, and rejected the values and aesthetics of both the punk scene and the commercial scene, standing on the far side of all those concepts, drunk and confused and perfectly confident and ready to play the next gig, but seriously questioning whether dying young and leaving a good-looking corpse is a meaningful pose any more. "Razzle dazzle drazzle drone/time for this one to come home/razzle dazzle drazzle die/time for this one to come alive." Maybe the apocalypse (personal or collective) is just another taken-for-granted value that's gotten old and flashy and false and needs to be resisted. Westerberg might not mind puking to death ("down on

all fives/let me crawl"), but he'll never do it if he thinks
it's expected of him.

R.E.M. on the other hand confine their rebellion to
the rather formal (but strikingly effective) technique of
mumbling their songs, never printing a lyric sheet, and
designing their album sleeves, choosing photos etc, so
that as little as possible is revealed. This is good because their music is so achingly beautiful, so intelligent,
and so reassuring (the apocalypse is not an issue for
them, except in the sense that they comment on how
glorious it is to be falling at high speed through the
universe) (*Feeling Gravity's Pull,* for example) that only
their bull-headed obscurantism protects them from a
mass public that would cheerfully eat them alive. *Fables
of the Reconstruction* sounds magnificent on the compact disc player. This to me is the follow-up to and
evolution of the Byrds' *Younger than Yesterday* that I've
been waiting for for nineteen years.

I saw Pat Benatar in concert a few weeks ago, and she
was terrible. She did a good imitation of being a good
sport about going through the motions (energetically,
even) but the only feeling that came through was bitter
resentment, masterfully repressed. She seems to think
(having her husband be her producer and bandleader
may be part of the problem) that she has no choice but
to give people what they think they want. (Townshend:
"I was bitter during the last five years of the Who because I felt that I couldn't get out. It seems very strange
in retrospect because I now realize I could've gotten
out at any time.")

The odd thing is that her 1985 single *Invincible,* which
apparently she only put on her album because the
record company insisted, is a performance I really like

(maybe it's not so odd; why should her tastes and mine coincide, any more than her tastes and her mass audience's?). This is the kind of manufactured pop (Mike Chapman, producer; Holly Knight, lyricist) that breaks out of the mold and just sparkles, or maybe it stays in the mold and sparkles; anyway, it's fabulous. "We can't afford to be innocent/stand up and face the enemy/it's a do or die situation/ we will be invincible!" I know that doesn't exactly mean anything, but the stance is great: pure victim (little girl voice, lyrics like "won't anybody help us?") combined with pure bluster ("we've got the right to be angry"), soaring vocals, and a relentless instrumental track. It's like the little mouse in the cartoons turning on the lion and saying, "C'mon. Put 'em up! Put 'em up!" We know the lion's going to run away, and the cute little mouse will blush and say, "Shucks, it was nothing." Benatar may not like this song, but she's still singing for me and every other rock fan. "This shattered dream you cannot justify/we're gonna dream until we're satisfied." Take that, you bully. We will be invincible. Rock and roll will never die, and so forth.

To be a rock and roll fan today is to have an enormous smorgasbord of music and related experiences to choose from. In many places you can just turn on the TV any time of night or day and have MTV or other music video channels in your face. Visual rock on tap. On the radio there's soft rock, hard rock for the youth demographic, hard rock for the 25-35 demographic, current hits, rock oldies, urban rock (mostly by black performers, a variation on the old r&b/soul formats), freaky underground stuff on college radio, and so forth. In the record store you'll find records, compact discs, cassettes (for your Walkman or boom box or car stereo or home dubbing deck), videocassettes (rent or buy), singles, twelve-inch singles, and probably books, t-shirts, magazines and posters. Dance clubs are everywhere, and if you live in or near a city, there are also lots of places to hear different kinds of live rock music, at clubs, concert halls, stadiums etc. In general there are so many records and videotapes and everything else that even if only five per cent of them were any good, you'd never have time to hear or see all the good ones. And the stuff comes in every imaginable rock flavor, from hardcore punk to syntho-pop to psychedelic country: you can pick and choose the styles, traditions, and attitudes that appeal to you.

This fragmentation into different categories began in the late Sixties, a natural outgrowth of the huge expansion of rock's audience at that time. It peaked in the mid-Seventies, when the different strains of rock seemed to have nothing in common but history. A Yes fan was not likely to be into Black Sabbath; Earth Wind & Fire's audience overlapped very little with Neil Young's. It was reasonable to think at the time that these very different musical genres were only lumped under the general heading of rock as a matter of inertia, and that before long the term would cease to have any meaning at all.

The 1980s have seen a process of reunification. The music is more varied than ever, and the size of the total audience is much larger than ever, but there's some sense of collective identity again. In the 1970s artists like Elton John, Rod Stewart, the Bee Gees, and Fleetwood Mac were extremely popular, but that in fact was their sole identifying characteristic: popular. There was a blandness at rock's center that made "pop music" seem a much more appropriate term. There were all these different categories of rock, but "rock" itself had no character. MTV has helped to change that (even though it excludes more than it includes). The Police, U2, Prince, Michael Jackson, and Bruce Springsteen symbolize a new generation of superstars who give rock some kind of musical identity and purpose again. *We Are the World* and Live Aid were made possible by this renewed sense of collective identity, and in turn have contributed tremendously to it. Live Aid was a reassertion of rock's identity — it may not have been intended as that, but it has certainly worked out that way.

So here I am at this 1986 smorgasbord. I just received in the mail two cassettes of U2 concerts, one a Denver appearance from their first U.S. tour in 1981, the other a Madison Square Garden show from spring 1985. Both tapes are terrific, and there's a lot more where these came from. As I listen to U2 live, their studio recordings also start appealing to me more, I suppose because I'm getting to know the songs better. They are portraits of the human heart in action, painted in bold, bright strokes, sloppy, committed, alive. Unafraid, unembarrassed, but not necessarily immodest. And the more I listen, the more moved I am, and the more I understand why people compare this band to the early Stones. They don't sound like the Stones at all, but they have that intensity, some kind of similar rock aesthetic — not who the Stones became but who they were when they were as young as U2 are now, what they stood for and how their songs felt to fans like me.

What kind of a fan am I today? In some ways I'm unchanged, and I still look for and sometimes find in the music exactly whatever it was I hungered after when I was sixteen (proof that the world is a passionate place; a friend in the lonely night; release for my anger, confusion, idealism, desire, fear and love). In other ways, I'm not the same, and can't be satisfied pretending I am. Don't even want to be. One thing I notice is, there may be as much great music around as ever, but these days I almost have to force myself to listen to it. My hunger is real, food is in front of me, but still I hesitate. What am I afraid of?

I like the way this flamboyant young Irishman, Bono, talks to his audience (me, even though I wasn't actually in Madison Square Garden that night) (imagine his clear, rich, forthright tenor): "It's taken me — it's taken me seven years to realize that, uh, you know, more important than all these amplifiers, more important than all this lighting above my head, more important than this whole building, are these four chords — that's a G, that's a D, I think that's an A-minor, and that's a C. Those four chords mean more than it all, because with those four chords you can write a song, a song like this one. A song, I didn't write it, and I, I dedicate it to the man who did. I also dedicate it to any other garage bands from garageland that are out there... because the songs, the songs will be your record company, the songs will be your agents, the songs will be your managers. So you find them first, okay?" And they start playing Bob Dylan's *Knocking on Heaven's Door.*

I read in *Rolling Stone* that Television was one of the bands that inspired U2 when they started playing together as teenagers, nine years ago. Television also used to do *Heaven's Door* as an encore. I'm thinking about digging through my boxes of cassettes to find my live Television tape. They were a great band. But they never got an album on the charts, whereas U2 sells in the millions. Among other things, that says something about the difference between the 1970s and the 1980s.

The rock fan I was before last summer, before my kids and Sting and Springsteen and *Shout* persuaded me that something was really happening, that present-day rock and roll was worthy of and would reward my full attention again, was a guy who didn't even have a phonograph any more and only listened to music when driving in the car, who would buy tapes not when something new came out but when he had to drive to L.A. or Seattle and didn't want to get bored on the way. And still I loved rock music, and searched for tapes that would excite me, satisfy, stimulate, make me happy — Buddy Holly's *20 Golden Greats* was a revelation for a while, and so was T-Bone Burnett's *Trap Door* and Bruce Cockburn's *Dancing in the Dragon's Jaws* and Talking Heads' *Speaking in Tongues*. And I'd make compilation tapes now and then, new and old favorites mixed together, often an unconscious statement of what was going on in my life as I chose the songs. I have one here I made four years ago — one side is called *Fountain of Sorrow,* and includes *Fountain of Sorrow* (Jackson Browne, 1974), *Section 43* (Country Joe & the Fish, '67), *Satisfaction* (the Rolling Stones, '65), *Trap Door* (T-Bone Burnett, '82), *I Wish You Could Have Seen Her Dance* (T-Bone Burnett, '82), *Heart of Mine* (Bob Dylan, '81), and *Jesus* (Velvet Underground, '69). The other side is *Ain't That Peculiar: Ain't That Peculiar* (Marvin Gaye, 1965), *Hospital* (the Modern Lovers, circa '72), *Poetry* (T-Bone Burnett, '82), *Things We Said Today* (the Beatles, '64), *Don't Doubt Yourself, Babe* (the Byrds, '65), *Watching the Wheels* (John Lennon, '80), *Walking on Thin Ice* (Yoko Ono, '81), and *Gates of Eden* (Bob Dylan, live in Europe 1978). Wonderful tape.

I just found out, by looking in the dictionary, that what I mean by the word "apocalypse" is different from any of the published definitions. The dictionary defines it as a revelation, a disclosure, and also as an alternate name for the Book of Revelation in the Bible. This latter explains where the vernacular sense of it that's been in my consciousness since at least 1967 comes from — to me the apocalypse is the end of the world, or, more subjectively (and thus offering great metaphoric possibilities), the end of the world as we know it. Noah's flood was an apocalypse, and the image of Gabriel blowing his horn and the dead awakening is utterly apocalyptic, and brings up the point that there can be such a thing as a joyous apocalypse. In fact, I've always associated the word "apocalyptic" with a kind of expectancy and anticipation, acknowledging the human desire for some sort of dramatic event of a scope much grander than our everyday struggles, which will somehow resolve or release these mundane entanglements (perhaps at the cost of everything we hold dear, which is the paradox, and explains why there's a kind of guilty pleasure in this sort of fascination and anticipation).

I remember feeling it was anything but a coincidence when Manfred Mann's version of Dylan's *The Mighty Quinn* hit the top ten in March of 1968. The rock and roll/alternative press/ antiwar/psychedelic drug culture that I was immersed in at the time was (it seemed to me) more and more caught up in visions of the apocalypse every day. I can remember the previous summer staring at a headline on the *New York Post* at the tail end of a powerful LSD trip: the headline said, "RIOTS SPREAD TO 30 CITIES," and below it was a quote from Robert Kennedy saying this was the worst crisis in our nation's history since the Civil War. That November I took part in the siege of the Pentagon — the image that remains in my mind is sitting on the ground linking arms with other protesters, facing Army Airborne troops who had loaded rifles with fixed bayonets pointed at us, garbage fires burning within the occupied areas of the Pentagon steps and parking lots behind us. It was a cold night. February brought the Tet offensive, and then LBJ resigned (my friends and I got that news after walking out of a showing of *The Battle of Algiers*), and then Martin Luther King was shot. The following night I was in the Fillmore East, stoned and paranoid, the Who were on stage and I was sitting there expecting someone to drive by (there were riots in the Bronx) and throw a Molotov cocktail into the theater. When Townshend and Moon trashed their guitar and drums at the end of the show, it was anticlimactic.

So "everybody's building ships and boats" and "when Quinn the Eskimo gets here..." sounded to me like acknowledgment, not of the coming apocalypse itself, but of this environment of all these people around me constantly (covertly and overtly) expecting the apocalypse, waiting for the next bigger maybe final shoe to fall, the revolution as a kind of ultimate riot (same feeling this very week in the Philippines as I write) or else some unexpected drama even greater than the dramas that had been piled one on top of the other for the last many months. One gets addicted to a certain kind of thrill. I appreciated that Dylan could (in my interpretation) be ironic about it, see the humor in our obsessions.

And by extension I guess any helplessly dramatic sense of impending doom or revelation, any sort of big event that happens to *everybody* (not just some people) all at once, makes me think "apocalyptic," "apocalypse." Tramaine's *Fall Down* has an apocalyptic quality because she communicates to me that she anticipates the spirit of love falling down on all of us at once, dramatically and unmistakably, the end and the beginning, not just a little kiss of God energy to start off her day. But that doesn't mean I hear the song as being narrowly about that—it's also about joy, private joy, any experience of renewal and/or God intoxication, and certainly it's also very sexual ("fall down/on me/let your spirit fall down on me"). Good sex is apocalyptic: this is *it*. Ecstasy and speaking in tongues and visions of the sky cracking open as He returns are closely related I think, and show up in our day-to-day lives primarily in sex and in music. Sex, music, and religious awe have never been separable since any of the three were invented.

I speak of the Replacements' *Hold My Life* in terms of a sort of agnostic search for an appropriate stance towards the apocalypse because I believe that for any one of us anticipation of the end of this world and of one's own personal death are essentially the same thing: objectively the world may not die when I do but subjectively it's absolutely so. And my power to bring about this event by my own actions raises all kinds of spiritual questions, especially when one is stoned enough (on God or booze or creative energy) to go beyond mere fear. Lead singer Westerberg gargles in tongues at the beginning of the song, invoking some sort of guiding spirit; I think that same spirit is playing the *Eight Miles High* guitar riffs at the end of the take.

And what I'm saying about R.E.M. is that they project and express a world-view in which the apocalypse is constantly occurring. "No reason to get excited," therefore. The moment of truth is perpetually at hand.

Part of the excitement of *When Doves Cry* is that it was a number one song almost from the moment that any of us first heard it. That's collective experience. I say my stepson Erik understands rock and roll because his comment goes directly to what is most significant and dramatic about this music: its ability to promote simultaneous experience by large parts of the collective human entity. It educates that collective being Teilhard de Chardin spoke of, by giving us experiences of functioning as one, and thus plays an important role in our mass awakening. It allows us (moments of) awareness of ourself.

Perhaps a taste of the apocalyptic is an essential quality that can be found in all rock and roll. That is, inherent in this music is the feeling that something big is going to happen, and that this song, this performance, exists in relation to that moment: announces it, brings it closer, expresses desire for or fear of that moment, comments ironically on it, attempts to avoid it, etc. You won't always find this in the lyrics, of course. In the case of Elvis, the apocalyptic quality is primarily in his voice, no matter what he's singing about: he makes you feel that reality just moved three steps closer, it's unsettling, always exciting. And then *Heartbreak Hotel* or *Jailhouse Rock* are examples of songs that are explicitly apocalyptic ("everybody in the old cell block/doing the jailhouse rock" might have been funny if the Coasters had sung it, but from Elvis it conjures up images of the whole human race busting out of our prison, someday soon). With the Stones, the guitar riff is the thing: the riff itself is ominous, the relentless repetition of it becomes apocalyptic. And explicitly, there's *(This Could Be) The Last Time* or *Paint It Black* or *Gimme Shelter* or *Midnight Rambler* ("everybody's got to go"), although to me the Stones doing *Mona*, a Bo Diddley cover with perfectly innocuous lyrics, is about as magnificent an evocation of the next-to-last trembling second of recorded time as anyone could ask for. Without even putting the record on, just thinking about it, I can feel it shuddering in every drop of blood in my body. (Bo's original is almost equally primal, if you can lay your hands on a copy.)

The music I loved in the '70s (Springsteen live doing *Incident on 57th Street,* Patti Smith's *Gloria,* Neil Young bootleg live *See the Sky about to Rain,* Anita Ward's *Ring My Bell,* Bob Marley & the Wailers' *Exodus*) had this quality, but what was lacking for me was a sense of belonging. The Sex Pistols brought it all together for half a moment, but most of the time everything just seemed to be going in different directions. I didn't feel any sense of collective motion, or else I did now and then and then felt let down when I discovered I was kidding myself, trying to relive past glories.

Music became a consolation prize instead of a common banner. And what is it now? I see myself getting excited, and I get suspicious. "Won't get fooled again. Oh no!" "Won't get fooled again. Oh no!" "Won't get fooled again. Oh no!" The aftermath of '60s idealism is a deep-seated cynicism that wells up like a broken record. All I want from music is to be part of (the illusion of?) a mass movement again that is out on the edge and really means something—a consciousness movement, not mere politics or culture or sex or aesthetics or any of those incomplete realms.

I think I hear the pied piper again, and what I'm afraid of is I might be wrong.

And the other thing I'm afraid of is I might be right.

Chapter Four

"Yeah we're on our way/and we can't turn back."
— The Doors

I'm sitting here in hog heaven, after a visit to The Last Record Store. The great Northern California floods of 1986 had pretty much confined me to my hometown for a week or more, so I was ready for a shopping spree in Santa Rosa. As it worked out I only had an hour, but a lot can be done in a short time if your need is great enough ("I wonder often what the vintners buy one-half so precious as the stuff they sell").

The Last Record Store is one of those eternal watering holes (with any luck you have one in your neck of the woods) where the spirit of rock and roll and related musics is kept alive, nourished, and dispensed to the needy. Usually, as in a good bookstore, there's this person behind the counter who is both knowledgeable and opinionated. I've been going to stores like this since I first earned any money babysitting, and when I'm the least bit open to it they never fail to plug me in to what's new in my kind of music (even when I'm not sure what kind that is, these days). House of Oldies in Greenwich Village used to help keep *Crawdaddy!* in touch in our early days in New York. Briggs & Briggs in Harvard Square was my hangout in my folk/blues era, and when I got into the Stones there was this guy behind the counter named Jon Landau who was as excited about *Have Mercy* as I was. Later I started a magazine and got him to write some reviews for it. Today he's Bruce Springsteen's manager and record producer; and probably he still goes down to the local hip record store when he wants to find out what else is happening in rock and roll.

So here's what I came out of The Last Record Store with: three albums, five compact discs, and a ticket to a show at the Cotati Cabaret. (I also picked up a free copy of a local music magazine, *BAM*, and afterwards I went to the newsstand next door and bought the latest *Billboard* and *New Musical Express*, music industry publications from the U.S. and the U.K., respectively, both of which I've been gleaning information from for more than two decades, whenever I've gone into one of these intensive rock phases.)

How does one find out what's new and exciting before it hits the cover of *Newsweek* or *Rolling Stone*? Okay, here's an example. I met a guy in a coffee house in San Francisco, and we ended up going to his apartment so I could see a Bob Dylan record I don't have, and he played me part of a new album by someone named Mojo Nixon. (This guy, Adam Block, happens to be a rock writer, and I met him because I was hanging out with some friends from a radio station and he knew them, so this is kind of in-group —but it doesn't matter, you can meet people anywhere who'll turn you on to new music if you're willing to listen.)

I liked the record, so I looked for it at my local store, couldn't find it, and asked the owner. He said it was sold out, and was I going to the show? Which is how I found out that Mojo Nixon and another much-talked of new item, the Beat Farmers, are playing in Cotati, over the hill from my house, this Thursday. The record store guy was telling everybody about this show, he's a fan of both these acts. So I guess I might have found out about it anyway. And then I notice that in an interview with R.E.M.'s guitarist Peter Buck in the current *Record* magazine, he cites the Mojo Nixon and Skid Roper album as his choice for recommended new platter ("sounds like a combination of Jonathan Richman and John Lee Hooker on mushrooms"). This is how it works – all you have to do is put yourself in the line of fire, go to the store or skim the magazines or talk to people or listen to the radio or something, and if you can just keep a lid on your attitudes and be open to the possibility that there might be something new and worthwhile out there that you don't already know about, it'll seek you out from all directions.

A lot of what I bought is stuff I'd never heard before. I've been hearing about Hüsker Dü in every magazine, every critics' poll; I asked the record store guy which of their recent albums was better, and he pointed me real clearly to *Flip Your Wig*, he didn't even like the other one. Later I might find I have the opposite view, but at least it gives me a place to start. My old friend Sandy Pearlman mentioned Green on Red to me some months ago, and I've been eyeing their records and watching to see if they play a local club – finding a used copy of one of their albums was enough to get me to take a chance on them finally. The other LP I purchased was U2's live mini-album *Under A Blood Red Sky*, which I've also had my eye on for months.

The worst thing about the compact disc player is the price of the discs — I can't afford 'em but they sound so great I can't resist 'em either. The Last Record Store had just gotten in a large selection of used CDs (just like new — you can't scratch 'em!), and I bought the Doors' first album, which I've been looking for on CD, and three other classics: *Who's Next*, Talking Heads' *Little Creatures* (instant classic), and Pink Floyd's *Dark Side of the Moon*. The latter I've never really been into, having skipped most of what was big in the '70s, but Translator's drummer Dave Scheff was with me when I bought my CD player in New York, and commented that that would be the first disc he'd buy. I passed on it then, but his comment stayed with me. It's not only new stuff one has to have an open mind about.

I also picked up a CD copy of Lone Justice's first album, another new group I've been hearing a lot about. I like the idea of being introduced to something via CD, instead of by lp or cassette.

The next challenge is to find time to listen enough, given that it's always taken me a lot of exposure to anything really new before I start feeling it, connecting with it, speaking its language. Money and time are big considerations when it comes to exposing oneself to current music, and that means commitment. What happens to a lot of us as we get older, I think, is that our commitment to rock and roll or new music starts to diminish, a perfectly normal process (there are other things in life), but then there's this downward spiral:

the less time we have to listen and the fewer albums or shows we risk, the fewer discoveries we make, and so we listen even less.

The way to turn this around, if one wants to, is not to sit and wait for the perfect group or the perfect album — which anyway, whether one realizes it or not, is a projection of old standards, values, memories, and therefore a) will never exist and b) wouldn't sound new if it did — but to jump in with both feet to whatever seems interesting right now.

I've been hanging out with this group Translator at various times in the last few months in order to observe not the band per se but something that I call the process of rock and roll. It's been a lot of fun, mostly I suppose because these guys are fun people to be with, and because I like the music they make. If I didn't like the music, mixdown sessions where one listens to the same song (or parts of the same song) forty times in a row would probably have been less enjoyable, and if the people in the band weren't fun to be with, eight days of sleeping on the floor of their hotel suite (I went to New York with them for the mixdown) and of getting up at four in the afternoon and going to sleep at eight or nine in the morning might have gotten a little tiresome. As it was, we had a very pleasant time, without resorting to any vices more extravagant than the occasional joint, good food, and the daily two-mile walk at dawn back to the hotel from the studio.

Back in March of 1967, a few months after *Crawdaddy!* and I moved from Boston to New York City, Murray the K put on what was to be the last of the great multi-talent rock/pop disc-jockey-produced stage shows, at RKO's 58th Street Theater in New York. It was spring

vacation — the show ran for a week, starting each morning at ten, five continuous shows every day with each act
playing for ten or twenty minutes at a time. The head-
liner this year was Mitch Ryder, and the other acts included Wilson Pickett, Smokey Robinson & the
Miracles, the Blues Project, Cream, and the Who. The
latter two groups were making their first American appearances.

I hung out backstage a lot, clowning around with
Entwistle, Moon, Clapton, Al Kooper, Ginger Baker,
Wilson Pickett's band, and so forth, chatting with Pete
Townshend about science fiction. The rest of the gang
from *Crawdaddy!* came and went as well. There were
moments in the show that you'd drag yourself out of the
dressing rooms to catch each time — Jim & Jean singing
Changes, Pickett's *Midnight Hour,* the Who doing *Happy
Jack* and *My Generation.* But it all ran together, and so
much of it was bad — the Blues Magoos and a number of
other pseudo-psychedelic bands were on the bill — and
the Blues Project and Cream had a very tough time
playing ten-minute sets to teenyboppers who didn't
want to hear them, through a dubious sound system,
five times a day, and so none of us really took it like an
opportunity for good music; instead it was a nonstop
backstage party, the usual attempt on the part of the
musicians and hangers-on to disguise from ourselves
the fact that we were mostly bored out of our skulls.

Actually it's all pretty vague in my mind, memory
being what it is, and what stands out clearest is a gag a
bunch of us got into. Every time Mitch Ryder's band
(he'd just broken up with the great Detroit Wheels,
alas, and had some pick-up soul band instead) went
onstage they played this rinky-dink version of the horn

riff from Sam & Dave's *Hold On, I'm Coming*...DA DA
dum dum da da DA...over and over, it didn't seem to
matter what song was actually coming up, and so backstage some of the other musicians, Brits especially,
started bursting into a vocal chorus of DA DA dum
dum da da DA whenever things got a little slow or a
spot of humor seemed otherwise called for. Like any
standing gag, it got riotously funny, but you had to be
there.

Hanging out with Translator while they mixed down
their album *Evening of the Harvest* was more fun and
more exciting for me than hanging out with the Who
and Cream backstage during their first American
shows. That's in terms of how I felt in each case while it
was happening. Only time will tell whether the Translator sessions will someday have the kind of aura about
them that the Murray the K gig does now that the Who
and Cream are certified rock legends. There's a sort of
"historic" excitement that has very little to do with how
things feel in the moment. Anything, even Jack
Kerouac or Keith Moon passing out in a corner from
too much booze, can appear fabulously romantic when
seen through the rose-colored lenses of time and
mythic context.

What was exciting about the time in New York with
Translator wasn't what we actually did—a lot of the
time we just watched late night television while Ed
Stasium, the producer, worked on technical aspects of
the mixdown in the room next door. What was exciting
was how good the music was, how fabulous each track
sounded as we approached a final mix. It was a feeling
of artistic and professional satisfaction, mixed with anticipation: wait till they hear this!

I was alone with Ed at one point while he was mixing *You To Love,* working on the relationship between snare drum, bass guitar, and lead guitar, and getting great results. He looked up briefly from the computer-controlled playback and flashed a grin: "I'm on a roll." All I could say was, "Yeah!" He turned his attention back to the board and muttered, "I hope the rest of my life's like this."

When you're doing work you love to do, and that work is going well, when you're taking risks and they're paying off, there's no better feeling in the world. That's the feeling that pours off the stage on a good night with a good rock band: communicating the joy of communicating. People will put up with a lot of hassles and disappointments for a chance to get to that place again.

At the end of the mixdown, the last night in the studio, I recorded a short interview with Ed Stasium about his experience producing *Evening of the Harvest.*

Paul: "What happened before you came out [to California for the recording sessions]? You had some kind of input from CBS...". (Stasium is an independent producer, hired by the record company and the band to record this album.)

Ed: "Well, my attitude on first arriving in San Francisco from here was that they needed some — CBS had heard the demos [rough recordings of songs the band was considering for inclusion on the album], and Translator needed a hit single. Because that is basically CBS's philosophy, is making hit singles. I even went as far as writing a tune with a friend of mine to present to the band to do for this record. And I was going to go out there and try to see if we can work out, make this stuff more commercial, because CBS didn't think the demos were all that commercial – I liked them, but I did understand what CBS was saying.

"But once I got into rehearsal with the band, I saw that indeed what they were doing was just as much commercial as, you know, Starship doing *We Built This City,* in their own way. Well, not really, because that was a blatantly manufactured, a blatant attempt at making – a success at making a hit record.

"What really got to me was the fellows' attitudes – and I probably knew this the entire time before I went out there, but um, the guys are really into what they're doing. They're telling the truth in what they're doing. There's no bullshit involved. They're not writing songs to have a hit. They're writing songs about what they feel, and their life experience, and they play what they feel. They're not playing prescribed riffs that have been put out by the radio doctors out there, that have been being fed into people's brains for the last few years.

"They're playing what they feel, and that just, it gives me the chills every time I think about that, because it's great, that was my initial idea of what rock and roll was all about. It wasn't – well, for some people it's making a big buck, and striking it rich, and having a hit record, but for other people it's artistic gratification. I enjoy getting artistic gratification out of making a record, rather than sitting on it and saying, 'Oh man, this is a hit, I'm going to make millions and millions of dollars.' I certainly would like to make a lot of money, but – who cares, when you're making a record this great?

"God, it just came together so great. And compared to all the other records that are being made today, that spend six months or a year being made and putting every little piece of it together... This was done live, we

knocked the backing tracks off in four days, and did all
the overdubs in like twelve days, and mixed it in ten
days—we're talking about just a little over a month of
recording. Unprecedented. And to come out with a
product like this—it's fucking great."

Paul: "So you feel that it's very rare to work like this,
these days?"

Ed: "It's absolutely— I've never done it, and I've
made ninety records."

Paul: "So how did it come about that you did this one
this way?"

Ed: "That's what the band wanted to do. They said,
'We want to do this.' And I said, 'Let's rehearse a lot,
and get it right, and then go do it.' And we did it. With
the exception of the two solos, and some acoustic overdubs, and a couple of keyboards, the record's basically
live." (The band-members played their instruments
together at the same time in the same room...like a
stage performance, except in the studio. They also sang
as they played, but the vocals were rerecorded later
(overdubbed).)

Paul: "So in that sense it seems like a coming
together of things—what they wanted to do was in fact
something that you got tremendously excited about
doing."

Ed: "It's a challenge. Nobody does this. And I hope
it's a success, because I can, I hate to say it but, laugh in
some people's faces. People who are convinced that
they have to sit down and write hit material, and they
have to think about what the public will—'What do
they want to hear now?' And, 'what do they want to
hear next?' And, 'this sounds like it will catch the
public's eye.'

"But this is right from the heart. This was what I thought, this is what the public thinks record-making is all about to begin with. Most people do not know that what's on the record is not live, that ordinarily you start with a track, and build another track on it... But this one's really live. It's wild. It's like the '60s, it has that feeling, that '60s vibe to it. It's unpremeditated."

I got invited to be a guest disc jockey on a San Francisco radio station, KKCY, a few weeks ago – the show was *Critic's Choice,* I could play whatever I wanted and talk about it and so forth. I played a couple of songs from Translator, I played *Fall Down,* I played R.E.M. and U2 and the Replacements, I played a demo tape by my friend Sachiko, I played Bob Dylan and Los Lobos and Tears for Fears, and I fooled around with the compact disc player, comparing the Rolling Stones' *Honky Tonk Women* on CD and on the original 45 (the 45 is much better, partly I think because the CD was mastered wrong, but maybe also because there are certain limitations on digital sound in terms of reproducing the raw beauty and power of rock and soul singles). I also used the quick advance on the CD player to play the first five or ten seconds of every track on ZZ Top's new album. Fun.

Rock and roll is a loose medium, it's free-form, it's made for taking chances and having fun. In the '70s things got ridiculously organized and sanitized, and still today there's a lot of rigidity and sterility in different parts of the scene. Radio is 98% dreadful, with a few rays of light here and there suggesting that something new could be coming over the horizon. The record companies, to their credit, are putting out some excellent records; but it's also true that they're as greedy and short-sighted as they've ever been, maybe worse. Most people in the rock music business think they know how to "do" rock records or rock concerts, and that's deadly. There's a lot of pandering, a lot of corruption, a lot of so-called professionals who look down on the people they're serving. Which is perfectly normal, this has been the norm throughout rock's three decades so far. What's fascinating is that somehow the free spirit of rock and roll survives and keeps breaking through all the bullshit. If the money-machine could reduce it all to a safe, money-making formula, it would; but attempts to do that in the '70s ultimately created a severe recession in the record business, because the audience lost interest in the music.

Ed Stasium is right in saying that recording instrumental tracks live in the studio is seldom done any more, but there are some significant exceptions to this rule: Bob Dylan and Neil Young are two major artists who almost always record live, the tracks for Bruce Springsteen's *Born in the U.S.A.* were recorded live in the studio, and the Rolling Stones have attempted to return to their roots by recording parts of their new album the same way. The Replacements and many other not-yet-commercial bands record live for economic reasons as well as aesthetic ones, and this "sound" is getting more attention all the time. This could almost be a trend, were it not that 98% of what's on the Hot 100 Singles charts, and at least 80% of the top 50 albums, are made in the opposite fashion.

"Then I had another thought," writes Richard Feynman. "Physics disgusts me a little bit now, but I used to *enjoy* doing physics. Why did I enjoy it? I used to *play* with it. I used to do whatever I felt like doing — it didn't have to do with whether it was important for the development of nuclear physics, but whether it was interesting and amusing for me to play with." The Nobel prizewinning physicist is describing the first time he "burned out," at age 28. "So I got this new attitude. Now that I am burned out and I'll never accomplish anything...I'm going to *play* with physics, whenever I want to, without worrying about any importance whatsoever." Rock and roll, like theoretical physics, depends on inspiration and enthusiasm more than craft. I would guess that every rock musician, at the age of 22 or 32 or whenever it hits, comes up against this same wall, and either has this revelation and gets back to having fun, rocking, or fails to have it and gets buried under the weight of maintaining importance or stardom or chops.

Looking like you're having fun, by the way, can be as much of a trap for a rock and roller as "writing important lyrics," or whatever. You start to feel this sense of obligation. What once was a pleasure becomes a chore. The image of freedom sells records — "this guy really knows how to party!" — but it can become a prison, which means it could be the very thing that's keeping you from being free.

I taped an interview with Bruce Springsteen in 1974, at a time when CBS wanted to drop him from the label because he wasn't selling enough records, and we talked about a performer's ability to decide his own destiny.

Paul: "I sometimes wonder if the way that the record business is now can actually stop things from happening, just in the sense of stopping them from happening on the radio, or..."

Bruce: "Yes. I mean, it's like — First of all, only to a certain degree. I don't really want to get into the specifics, because I know some things that have been done to me, you know [laughs] and I don't want to sound like, I don't want to whine. But they could stop it to a degree. They can't stop you going out there and playing every night. They can't stop you from being good. They can keep it off the radio. They can make sure it gets low airplay, or no airplay, or whatever, which, it hurts, yeah. But they can't— well gosh, like, I've been playing, we've been going for two years, and the second record's the biggest, it's sold what, 70,000? That's nothing. That's zero. And I don't know, I don't think they can —

"It depends on who they're dealing with, who they're messing with. It depends on the person, it's like anything. Some people can be stopped, and other people can't be stopped, you know? It depends, if you're dealing with people who *can* stop, or not. Like me, you know, I can't stop, they can't make me stop, ever. It's like once you stop, that's it. You might as well... I don't know what I'd do.

"But it's like that. If you're dealing with people who can say, 'Well, hell, I'm going to go back to, you know, hanging wallpaper [laughs], that was easier than this,' them you can stop. Those people who are going, 'Oh man, I'm gonna go back to college, forget this stuff,' those people can be stopped. People say, 'Hey, what should I do? Gee, I don't know if I want to play, or if I want to get married to my girl, I'm having a real hard time deciding...' Well, if you have to decide, the answer is right there: don't do it! If you have a choice, then the answer's no.

"It's only the ones who, some people really don't have a choice, and those are the people who – The record company, I don't like to use the term 'the record company,' cause they always get painted as the bad guys – it's like the pressures of the business, or whatever, are powerless in the face of what is real. [laughs] You just can't stop somebody with things like that. I don't think."

Paul: "Something that bothers me, but that you seem to have been able to get around pretty steadily, is the tendency for there to be nowhere to play except big arenas."

Bruce: "Well, it's simple. What you gotta do – Like, I did the Chicago tour, right? I did that tour because I had never played big places, and I said, 'Well, I ain't gonna say nothing, because I don't know what they're like.' So we went and played them. About fourteen nights in a row. Went crazy. I went insane during that tour, the worst state of mind I've ever been in, I think. And just because of the playing conditions for our band. The best part of the tour was the guys in Chicago, great guys, it was nice. But I couldn't play those big places, it had nothing to do with anything that meant anything to me, at all.

"Those big arenas. So I told Mike, 'I'm never going to play those places again.' And that was it. So he knows that usually we don't play any place over three thousand, that's the highest I like to go. I don't like to go any bigger than that. And that's even too big."

Paul: "The challenge comes when you get more popular, which is inevitable."

Bruce: "Right, you know, but – It's like, there's no way! I'm always disappointed in acts that play those places. I don't know how The Band can go out and play like that. I don't know how Joni Mitchell can do it. I don't know how you can play there. You can't. You can't effectively do it, I don't think."

Paul: "I guess it's because somebody — like the Who, you'd expect them to do different, but I guess what they'd have to do, really, would be to have somebody come in and book a concert hall in New York City — "

Bruce: "For a week."

Paul: "For at least a week. They're doing four shows in Madison Square Garden and it was sold out in an hour. So it would have to be at least a week of two shows a night, or maybe more."

Bruce: "Yeah, you gotta do that, and you also gotta realize that if you get that big, some people who want to see ya, ain't gonna see ya. See, I don't know, I'm not in that position, I don't know if I'll ever be in that position. All I know is, those big coliseums ain't where it's supposed to be, you know, it just ain't where it's supposed to be. It's just too big."

Paul: "It's always a drag, especially if you're not sitting in the front row."

Bruce: "Like I said, it's something else going on all over the room. You go to the back row, you can't see the stage, talk about see what's on it. All you see is a blot of light. You better bring your binocs, you know."

Paul: "I guess people go just for the event..."

Bruce: "See, it turns into — what happens is you go to those places and it turns into something else that it ain't. It becomes an event, rather than, I don't know, whatever else it is. It's just hard to play. But that's where everybody's playing, any more."

Paul: "It's the biggest part of the entertainment business, I mean bigger than movies, bigger than television, much bigger than records. Arenas...that's the biggest, in total dollar gross..."

Bruce: "I don't know how they do it, I don't know how you can even expect to do it in a place like that. Especially like, especially our band, it would be impossible to reach out there the way that we try to do."

Paul: "Oh yeah, I think so. What happens is you end up playing an imitation of yourself, that's the best that—"

Bruce: "It's like, forget it, you know. That's what happens. So you start being somebody you read about."

And of course it came to pass that in 1985 Bruce Springsteen and the E Street Band played show after show in baseball stadiums, in front of 50, 60, or 80 thousand people at a clip, and still lots of people who wanted to see them, didn't get to see them. And that's just how the wheel turns, one week you're a punk, the next week you're a cultural icon, next week maybe you're an old geezer talking about glory days. It doesn't matter. Fred Goodman said in *Billboard* of a Giants Stadium Springsteen show, "It was tough to shake the feeling that one was watching MTV with a live adjunct rather than a concert. But criticism on this level pales next to the stamina and energy offered by Springsteen and company. In performance, he is clearly setting the standard for everyone else to meet, and he is probably the only person who can best it."

So the man had the freedom not to be imprisoned by last year's vows. And on the other hand, who could begrudge any punk today for holding the attitude Bruce himself expressed so earnestly in '74?

Jump in with both feet – the rule applies to the performer as much as the listener. I think of the Who ferociously busting the barriers of Murray the K's silly stage show in '67, Springsteen and band making us laugh, cry, whoop and holler for two and a half hours nonstop in those 3000-seaters in '74, Ed Stasium behind the board for mix after perfect mix in Right Track studio for Translator in '86. I like an art form that keeps seducing me to rejoin the ranks of those who can't be stopped.

I like the Lone Justice album a lot, and Donna and I are going to go see them in a local club – ah, the good old days when you could see Lone Justice and Maria McKee performing in a club! – this Saturday night.

Chapter Five

"That word does not exist in any language."

— Talking Heads

"There is nothing quite as absurd as a rock concert. In terms of pop culture, it's recordings, not live performances, that leave a stamp on history. Video is slowly changing this scenario, arguably for the worse, but the value of the rock concert performance remains intact — it's nothing more than a marketing tool, and art rarely springs from marketing tools." So writes Eric Lefcowitz in *Calendar* magazine, March 1986.

I enjoyed seeing Mojo Nixon last night, but I felt that his act, which is very entertaining, kind of got in the way of his genius. The excitement of his first number, *Twilight's Last Gleaming,* which he sang/shouted with no mike, strumming an unplugged electric guitar, one leg twitching out madly and slamming the floor to establish the beat, a surprised audience around him holding our breaths to try to hear the inspired funny brilliant lyric imagery, admiring his sheer nerve and the places he was getting to with it—that excitement diminished for me as Mojo revealed himself as clever showman, audience laughing dancing and shouting along through *I Hate Banks, You're Gonna Eat Those Words, Mushroom Maniac* and so forth. It was much fun, but when he climbed onstage after *Gleaming* and said, "that's all you're gonna get of the 'sensitive' Mojo tonight," he was telling the truth. I wouldn't say this about just anybody, but I'd like to see Mojo (and washboard accompanist Skid Roper) in front of a hopelessly indifferent or hostile crowd. I suspect they can be incandescent when they're ignored.

The Beat Farmers are another jackpot in the dice throw of my rock and roll adventure. They blew me away. What a versatile, flexible, powerful medium rock and roll is! Same old set-up: four guys, playing lead, rhythm, bass guitar and drums; everybody sings except the bass-player. The rhythm guitarist, who looks like a leader—dark glasses and a wry, self-assured attitude—trades songs with the lead guitarist, whose personality makes less of an impression at first (something subtle about the guy, though; he grows on you). Bass-player looks weird, of course: introverted/extroverted, skinhead, muscle shirt, tatoos. Looks like he knows something. Half a dozen songs into the set, the big, soft-faced, leather-cowboy-hatted drummer waltzes to a stage front mike to become the unexpected star of the show, waving his full beer bottle wildly (he also tosses it up in the air, spinning, and catches it or not), as he sings raunchy funny charming stuff like *California Kid* and *Happy Boy* (for one number he went out and sat on the dance floor with a long mike cord and got the audience to sit down around him—just before that people were shouting for *Country Dick!* and I thought it was a song, but it turns out to be his stage name) in a tough teddy bear guy of a voice that reminds of W.C. Fields doing John Wayne and Willie Nelson but could only belong to the dirty-mouthed drummer of the Beat Farmers. Pure crowd-pleaser, but in this case it is a straight-ahead vehicle for the guy's talent, and wisely he never does more than one or two numbers at a time. The rest of the band are too magnificently cool playing back-up to ever be upstaged (one or the other guitarist sits in at drums).

But there's plenty more here than this gorgeously lovable surprise hunk of showmanship. The songs are *all* good. It has to do with how they play together. Lots of acts I see lately I say, well, I'd probably have liked 'em a lot more if I'd been more familiar with their records. Never heard a note of the Farmers before, and couldn't pick up most of the lyrics or anything, but it didn't matter — the band works with my and their familiarity with the last fifty years of American music, rock country blues swing soul whatever you call it. Their music is heavily country-flavored, unquestionably rock, not hardcore punk in any sense but quite fluent with the aesthetic concepts thereof, comfortably drawing on the universal set of roots that underlies Beatles Elvis Springsteen Ramones Waylon Otis Replacements Los Lobos Motown and you name it. I wouldn't want to be the one to try to trace or identify the musical influences and specific threads, this is where I revert to idiot, like if you ask me what a chord is. But the Beat Farmers had already dazzled me with four or five tight, understated performances in a row, almost segued into each other (start of their second set), making reference through our shared musical language to a flood of feelings they know I know we have in common, when suddenly they played a song I'd heard before, *There She Goes Again,* from the Velvet Underground's first album. Country rock? Velvet Underground? It sounded part and parcel with all their other stuff, and it was a superb (again, understated) rendition. Later they grinned and did Neil Young's *Powderfinger.* This is a band after (and connected to) my own heart, and I'd go see them anytime.

Dissolve/reveal. Now it's Monday. I'm listening to the Stones' new single, *Harlem Shuffle.* I've seen two more shows since catching the Beat Farmers and Mojo Nixon Thursday night: Lone Justice at the Stone in San Francisco Saturday, and Black Flag (same club, very different audience) Sunday. I have a new star in my universe. Her name is Maria McKee.

When I heard Lone Justice's album I was very impressed, especially with the lead singer, who has a great voice and a lot of presence. I liked the songs, and was knocked out by the energy of the hard rock numbers (*East of Eden, Ways to Be Wicked, Wait Till We Get Home*). Even the more overtly country numbers appealed to me. So I was excited to discover, practically the first day I was listening to the album, that Lone Justice would be performing locally the following weekend. (Me being lucky again.)

The more I listened, the more excited I got. But I still wasn't prepared for the show I went to Saturday night. Maria McKee is a powerhouse performer, who at this stage in her career anyway is totally present in and totally committed to every word she sings and every movement she makes on stage. She sings with the kind of ease and speed Mick Jagger and Lou Reed had early in their careers, and she relates to her audience with the nonstop intensity and affection of Janis Joplin at her peak. Comparisons are dangerous, and I'm not necessarily saying she's as good as those people – in fact, I wouldn't even know how to measure such a thing. But subjectively, my experience standing in the audience (on the dance floor, three or four heads back, maybe ten feet from the edge of the stage) was like my experience watching Jim Morrison in 1967 or Bruce Springsteen in 1973 or Janis Joplin New Year's Eve 1967 at the Ark in Sausalito. I was transfixed. I was filled with joy. And I was startled awake once again by the news that there is something bigger than me in this world, and I can be a part of it. I got caught up in the performer's love of performing, her passion for reaching out through rock and roll.

Although there's a very strong country flavor to the album (balanced against an equally strong, almost contradictory rock flavor, creating an interesting tension), Lone Justice's show in San Francisco was rock all the way; the only overtly country aspects were a couple of ballads from the album included in the encores (great stuff), and Maria's stage persona, which is definitely country girl (cotton dress, she rolls her eyes a lot, comes on like a scrapper, calls her man "honey" and affects just a touch of a drawl). The covers they sang that I recognized were the Rolling Stones' *All Down the Line* (absolutely smokin', and a great choice), John Fogerty's *Fortunate Son* (sung with an unexpected and heartfelt anger that transformed it from a rockin' oldie to a powerful, very timely political statement), Janis Joplin's *Cry Baby* (she pulled it off; the woman has guts *and* style), and again, the Velvet Underground: climax of the first encore, a version of *Sweet Jane* (incorporating the audience singing the background bit from *Walk on the Wild Side,* incredible) that stands easily with any *Sweet Jane* I've ever heard. Then there were the originals, like her wonderful soliloquy with gospel quotations in the middle of *Soap, Soup and Salvation,* and another audience response bit, in *Wait Till We Get Home,* unlike anything I've experienced before – she had us chanting over and over "wait till we get home!" and then, us still chanting, she starts in on us, *"you're* telling *me* to 'wait'?!" Her presence is so strong she could get us singing not with her but against her, making us the son-of-a-bitch she's rebelling against, and keep us singing while she let us have it. Whew.

I'm still listening to *Harlem Shuffle,* and it's sounding better all the time. I've given up on the Rolling Stones and kicked their asses out of my life more times than I can count, but this is promising.

The Maria McKee I saw the other night was totally at home in the drama of her moment. When that happens to a performer, all the doors of creativity fly open. You get to a place (temporarily) where everything you try succeeds. All you have to do is throw your entire heart into it, give it everything you've got, spend all your love, trust, energy and talent right now. Believe that there's more where that came from, and if there isn't, at least you'll go out with a bang!

She's got this voice, and knows how to harness it with her band, on a rock and roll stage, and she has the ability to invent a role for herself and play it to the hilt, incorporating everything she's feeling and all the drama of the audience's hopes and expectations into each gesture, each phrase, each guitar chord. Part of how she does this is by being smart, and part is by being gifted, and part is by being lucky and in the right place at the right time, and part is by surrendering to the spirit. The greatest performances are channelled; the greatest performers are those who know how to stand in such a way that the lightning will strike and pass through them.

The only way I have of measuring a performance is subjective: after seeing Lone Justice perform, I feel like I'm living for the chance to see them again. And that's what I want from rock and roll. I want the shows and records to be so good that it's worth staying alive just to experience them.

Black Flag didn't move me to quite that degree, but I can see how they might have. They definitely got my attention. There were four guys — I expected more, some- how — and the singer, Henry Rollins, is a very powerful presence. He's tall, well-built, performed wearing noth- ing but black nylon boxer shorts (an elegant multicolor tattoo of the sun covers his back, with the words "search & destroy" above it), when he wasn't singing he had his lips pursed angrily, always looking like he was about to spit on the audience (he did spit, frequent- ly, but always back into the stage). While the music raged away behind him — drums, bass, electric guitar, and they were very good; I suppose some of the heavy metal bands may play this well, but it's been impossible for me to tell at arena volumes with arena acoustics — he would stand at stage edge, microphone constantly gripped in his left hand, riding the music, moving his body hypnotically, not for the audience seemingly but rather as an acknowledgment of and response to the physicality of the music. He had the dignity and grace certain large simians in the zoo achieve, looking out at the gawking crowd with both hostility and a kind of distant compassion, as if aware that his suffering must be nothing compared to theirs. Between songs when people called out requests and other comments, he would lean forward, make eye contact, and move his lips, "muh muh muh muh muh," mimicking them, communicating, "this is what you sound like to me." Always wary, but also in a strange way very giving; not holding himself back.

Black Flag is a hardcore band, which is what punk has evolved or devolved into, and as others have pointed out this music and heavy metal are definitely converging. But heavy metal is all pose and gesture; everything is formalized, and it seems to work best when the band is big enough to draw a large crowd, creating a sort of Nuremberg rally comraderie (not that I regard heavy metal music as essentially fascist; it simply draws on the same human instincts, as do many rock shows, and, significantly, uses them for celebration — and profit-taking — rather than for political ends). (I have to add that I haven't seen a heavy metal show in a club or small theater; possibly that would give me a whole other perspective.) Hardcore, on the other hand, is, at least in Black Flag's hands, a passionately sincere music. The loud guitar playing and the singer's screaming and sinuous movements are not formalized gestures intended to provoke ritualized responses, but rather an invocation of the dark muse, a spiritual and artistic and, often, political undertaking meant to call forward something wild and unknowable, something real and awakening and substantial in a dull and meaningless universe.

The audience at this show were not, for the most part, uniformed punks in mohawks and leather or skinhead regalia. It was a heterogenous crowd, and if a lot of them were fans of the band, they were careful not to be obvious about it. There was plenty of slamdancing immediately in front of the stage, and people did dive off the stage into the crowd — I got hit pretty hard on the side of the head at one point, when I was watching the dancing from the side (actually it attracted me, but I was unwilling to throw myself into the fray with my glasses on) and forgot to protect my flank. The slamdancing, in which people assault each other in a rough but impersonal, non-hostile, mostly fun-loving way, careening into their neighbors or sending others off with furious shoves, is exciting for the participants (like a barroom brawl but safer; people are usually quick to help you up and protect you if you fall) and also creates an atmosphere of danger for the crowd as a whole, since people may come flying into you at any time wherever you stand on the sidelines. This reduces the distance between performers and audience — both are at risk in an unstable situation — even though on another level it can serve as a huge distraction. It's a fascinating phenomenon, far from harmless but also more fun than you might think, and worth experiencing if you get a chance and you dare.

But for Black Flag, I'm sure, the slamdancing is just another familiar piece of the environment, like urine-soaked alleys in back of urban clubs, not necessary to their art but not inappropriate either. What impressed me about the band, besides the power of the music and

Rollins's striking visual and aural presence, was their
evident commitment. I know they've been touring tire-
lessly, year in and year out, and while I trust that their
hard work does earn them a little money (the show was
not that well-attended, actually, maybe partly because
the hardcore scene in San Francisco is being harassed
and is starting to fall apart), it was clear to me watching
them perform that what this is for them is a way of life
and an artistic quest, they look like they live to play
together on stage and that each night arrives as an opportunity to explore this thing a little further.

And their commitment is seductive. A lot of avant
garde artists beat the same old ideas to death endlessly
and act like they're doing something important. Black
Flag, on the other hand, strike me as real musicians and
real risk-takers; I can see myself wanting to experience
their show again before long, for the loud crashing
angry fun of it and also to find out how much further
and it what direction their hungers have taken them.

¤

The role of live performance in rock and roll is a fascinating, slippery subject. I wrote a whole book about
rock (*Outlaw Blues*, published in '69) in which I barely
mention any live performances. That's mostly because I
couldn't figure out how to write about them—with an
album you can discuss the songs track by track, and the
person reading either already is familiar with the album
or can go out and buy it if they want to, so there's this
common reference point. But with a show, by the time
you're reading about it it's over, and either you were
there or you weren't. I stuck to records, because I got
off on the idea of comparing notes with my readers on
experiences we'd been through together.

It's interesting to me that rock and roll may be the first music that originated and to a significant extent has been propagated as a recorded music rather than a performance music. Recorded music, after all, is something fairly new under the sun. Even in the twentieth century, the hit parade was based on sales of sheet music rather than records until the 1940s. Jazz and blues and pop music in pre-rock days were widely available on records, but these musical forms were still thought of in terms of a live music that could be captured on a recording. Rock and roll was something else. It didn't come out of the clubs or the concert halls or even live radio shows — people first encountered the concept of rock and roll through disc jockeys playing certain records, mostly selected rhythm & blues, and *calling* it rock and roll. Records were played on TV, and at record hops. The new stars did live shows, but they were recording artists first — it wasn't like there was a live rock and roll scene where talent was being discovered. The live form of rock was created after the fact, after the music established itself as an idea and a form through recordings.

I don't know. I wasn't there, and I'm not ready to go and research this thoroughly. I just have a strong feeling, which seems to be supported by the facts, that rock and roll is much more a recording-based music in its origins, and much less a music that springs from a live tradition, than any other music in human history.

But you know, I never felt satisfied about leaving live rock out of my book and my magazine. I discovered rock and roll through Rolling Stones and Kinks and Beatles records, but it wasn't long before I was mesmerized by the Blues Project playing at the Cafe Au

Go-Go, and then by the Doors and Jefferson Airplane and the Grateful Dead and Big Brother and the Who and so forth. There was an intensity in those live shows different from what I got from the records, just like I'd already felt something very different hearing Dave Van Ronk or Howling Wolf or Carolyn Hester live compared to listening to them on record.

And then I would hear phenomenal music that never seemed to make it onto disc — Moby Grape live were extraordinary, it seemed to me, but the album, while likable, barely hinted at that. Even Buffalo Springfield — even the Doors after their first album — were a disappointment on record compared to what I got from them live. There was a group called the Candymen that blew us all away live when they came to New York in '67, but nothing came of that because they didn't do their own material and the album they put out was a bore. Later, in the '70s, there was Springsteen, who never came close on a record to the miracles he and his band performed at every single live show. It was two different things, live and recorded rock, but the recorded you could talk about, you could play on the radio, you could package and sell. Live stuff had a market too, but the really big market was, and with some exceptions still is, restricted to people who'd made it big on record and who were willing to put on a show that would reproduce the record live.

So I can understand the guy in *Calendar* magazine saying it's recordings, not live performances, that leave a stamp on pop culture history. But that isn't because live rock is absurd, by a very long shot. If it's true, it's more because there's something missing in our histories. As a guy who's writing about rock and who's been to some of the great shows of the past and who's having a few comparable experiences with today's live performers, I feel compelled to redress this matter somehow. And it's a challenge. Sometimes I feel like all I can say is, "This was an exciting show—go see it if you can." And that's not enough.

History, incidentally, is gossip. Tongues wag, and it becomes the gospel truth for centuries; but even the gospels were largely written by people who weren't there. Not that having been there is any guarantee of accuracy. In the end, we believe what we want to believe.

Will videos make a difference? I doubt it. Because all a video is is a different kind of live record. Let me rephrase this. Videos will make a big difference, just as live records make a big difference, but when the line is drawn between recorded music and live performance, videos will still be recordings. It's exciting that there are more and different ways to record, and clearly the intensity of live performance will reach more people now as a result of the video revolution. And maybe, on the negative side, people will feel less of a need to drag themselves to live shows when they can see the same bands in close-up on their 40" TVs, with laser-quality sound and picture. I don't know. I do know I'll still want to be out there in the audience trading energy with Lone Justice or the Grateful Dead or R.E.M. or whoever in the flesh, as long as that possibility is open to me.

Chapter Six

"The dream is over./What can I say?"

— John Lennon

There are moments on this rock journey when I feel totally overwhelmed by information. It's exhausting. The *I Ching* says, "Unlimited possibilities are not suited to man; if they existed, his life would only dissolve in the boundless." I think the person who wrote that had just come back from a visit to Tower Records.

Harlem Shuffle still hasn't gotten past the "promising" stage after a week on my turntable, and that's not good. I like the sound and I like the beat, and that counts for a lot — it clears the way for greatness, as it were. But it's like the door is open and nothing's walking through. I keep waiting for that moment, as with *Honky Tonk Women* and *Jumping Jack Flash* and *Satisfaction* and even *Tumbling Dice,* when the song will suddenly seem to sum up everything that's happening in my life right now, when some dumb line from the lyrics like "you've got to roll me" or "I just can't seem to

drink up my mind" (it helps to mishear the lyrics sometimes) will transform itself, with the help of the beat
and the mood and the great sound wrapped all around
it, into a shimmering revelation with at least a dozen
different meanings, some funny, some sexy, some deeply profound, all clearly aimed directly at me like the
guys were reading my mind, like they get the full
awesomeness and can speak the unspeakableness of
everything I'm going through. Expectations are traps,
but anyway that's the truth about how I feel about this
Stones single, it's good enough to remind me how great
they can be and to suggest they could still do it if they
cared at all; good enough to be played again and again,
nice sound and hope springs eternal. But you know
there's something unsatisfying about sitting here with
the door wide open and nothing coming in. Is it me?
Am I stuck in the past? Am I asking too much of this
group? Naw, they're just wankers who still know how to
turn a guy's head, but are too wasted and cynical and
(secretly) unsure of themselves to know what to do
once they've got his attention. Damn it, I've been suck-
ered again. (But maybe if I listen just a few more
times...)

There's a Grateful Dead lyric that says, "I need a
miracle every day," and that's absolutely my relationship with rock and roll. I saw Translator Saturday night
and they put on a good show. What a disappointment.
Don't do no good show for me, guys — if you're not willing to be fantastic, you may as well just kick it over and
be terrible, at least that way maybe something unexpected will occur.

So I'm searching through Tower Records looking for
a miracle, and I think maybe I found it: *Psychocandy*, by

the Jesus and Mary Chain. I'm listening to side one now for the second time in a row and I'm TURNED ON. But before I settled on my purchases (also got Tramaine's album, which is finally out, and *King of America* by Elvis Costello, plus new copies of *Spin* and *Rolling Stone* — gak, information overload, I got a stack of these things on the shelf behind me that's gonna fall over and crush me when the earthquake hits), I wandered the aisles confronted by my own confusion and mixed emotions and all my bloody ATTITUDES.

I'll give you an example. Sunday's paper just announced a John Cougar Mellencamp concert here next month, and I easily decide I want to go, I'm curious about performer and audience both and it'll be real appropriate to my journey. So I'm standing at the bin, holding his album which is on sale, $2. off normal price, thinking, hell, if I'm going to go see him, why not expose myself to his album first? Makes a lot of sense, and after all this is the only record on the critics' top five in the year-end *Rolling Stone* that I don't own. And I'm staring at the record, it's only six dollars, and I finally put it down again, I just can't do it. Maybe it's the guy's face. The lyrics are on the back and I look at them and that doesn't help. None of the songs from the album I've heard on the radio do much for me. I don't know. What it really is, I think, is that I hate to buy an album that I end up feeling lukewarm about, that sits around *my house*, one of two million copies sold so far, and doesn't get played. What I buy, what I own, says something about me. Self-image. I think I want to be the kind of guy who'd give John Cougar Mellencamp a fair chance, but I just can't make myself do it.

So that's me up against my attitudes. I don't feel I made the wrong decision, necessarily – this book would get real tedious if I were writing it in the mood of someone who's forced himself to listen to everything everyone else likes, Mr. Fairness – but I don't enjoy going through the record store experiencing these little confrontations, thank you. Then on the information overload level, it's like: the Meat Puppets. I've seen a number of good mentions of the Meat Puppets. And they'll be in town next week. But I don't know. And anyway, which record? Exactly the same story with Robyn Hitchcock. He sounds *very* interesting, I think I want to see him, but would I like his records? Echo & the Bunnymen, same story. Here's the new Violent Femmes, produced by Jerry Harrison of Talking Heads. Never heard this group either, but hear of 'em a lot. I'll get it someday, but not today, I decide. (Since then I see them compared to two of my favorites, Velvets and Modern Lovers; comparisons are odious, but the Femmes are creeping up my list and will probably get bought on the next expedition.) And so forth and so on. Elvis Costello's new record, produced by T-Bone Burnett, seems a natural, but my problem there is my idiot stuff – somehow I've gotten to be 37 years old without ever listening to Elvis Costello, except the first time he was on *Saturday Night Live*, and once I saw a video of one of his songs. Where've I *been*?? It's embarrassing. So do I dare start listening now, twelve albums too late to be hip or even know what's going on, maybe? Well, I picked up late on Talking Heads (*everybody* tried to get me to listen to 'em from '75 on, but I wasn't going for it, just dug in my heels, I don't even know why, didn't break down till 1983), and that worked out. I pick up the Costello record. I'm looking for Green on Red but the album I want is sold out. I consider a Hendrix compact disc but it doesn't have quite the right songs on it. I consider *Big Audio Dynamite* again — no, the hell with it, I've got to get out of here......

A friend said he saw me on *Friday Night Videos* last week. Apparently they've made an after-the-fact video of John Lennon's *Give Peace A Chance,* edited from the Canadian TV footage of John & Yoko's "bed-in" in Montreal, and there I am singing out of tune and clapping my hands with the Hare Krishnas and Tim Leary and everybody. I've never seen the footage myself, but it's nice to be part of history (like the guy who shouted "Whipping Post!" on the Allman Brothers' *Live at the Fillmore* album). I can also be seen talking to somebody backstage for a few seconds in the *Woodstock* movie, and dancing crazily to Howling Wolf in the film about the Newport Folk Festivals.

The story about *Give Peace A Chance* is, I was travelling with Timothy and Rosemary Leary at the time; Tim was supposedly running for Governor of California, and my role for the week was campaign adviser. The first thing we did, after speaking to a college audience in San Luis Obispo, was fly to Hollywood, Florida for a rock festival on an Indian reservation, organized by the acid-dealing children of the Miami Mafia. The musicians and speakers never got paid (the Grateful Dead put on a great show anyway), but we managed to get plane tickets to New York, where Tim gave a press conference and introduced me to prospective campaign contributors as the hippie son of (then-unmarried) Canadian premier Trudeau.

We found out about the bed-in and wanted to go; a few phone calls later *Playboy* magazine agreed to pay our fare from New York City to Montreal on the condition that I record this historic first meeting between Leary and Lennon so it could be an interview or story in the magazine.

My recollection is that John and Yoko started their "bed-in" (they had already done the one in Amsterdam) in Toronto, ran into some kind of problem, and moved it to Montreal. At any rate, we met them in Montreal; they were in bed, in a large hotel suite. CBC (Canadian Broadcasting) was filming the event, and Derek Taylor, who had long worked for the Beatles and who I knew from his publicist days in LA, was serving as Master of Affairs for John and Yoko, handling details and crises and quietly making it all work. John was having a great time, in his element, the center of attention, talking on the phone to various radio stations around North America, plugging their new record (*The Ballad of John and Yoko,* with the controversial chorus, "Christ you know it ain't easy...they're gonna crucify me") and answering questions.

Yoko seemed shy and mainly talked to John; John was friendly, approachable, he seemed very real (that strange moment when the image of "John Lennon, Beatle" gives way to an actual person like any other person, there in front of you, saying hello, thinking whatever he's thinking, shaking your hand). The daytime was a circus of activity, with no opportunity for real personal communication or connection — there was always someone new coming in, some disc jockey calling or visiting, some new focus for John's attention, and he was a past master of being totally there and at ease with a new person every minute or three, "Hello, yes, this is really John Lennon, are you playing the record?"

While we were there a variety of celebrities came and went. Tommy Smothers was around, and also sang on *Give Peace A Chance.* CBC flew Al Capp, creator of *L'il Abner* and an outspoken critic of hippie and New Left politics, in to meet Lennon, to make their documentary a little more lively. Leary knew Capp from previous co-appearances ("debates") on the late '60s media circuit, and they got along well. Capp was very friendly to Leary personally, while making typically abrasive, very negative comments on Leary's "constituency." Leary grinned, disagreed wittily, but never took it personally.

Lennon, on the other hand, was really flustered when Capp started in on him. The Capp/Lennon exchange was at bedside, on camera, and Capp was playing for the viewing audience at home. Lennon had lived his recent life in public and before the cameras—even his honeymoon—but as a pop star I suspect he'd been fairly well protected from people attacking or criticizing him face to face. The bed-ins marked his first direct move into the political arena...he was making a public statement about peace, and that made him a politician, and the rules of that game are very different from the rules of "pop star."

So Capp came in to the bed-in circus, met John and Yoko, and after the introductions he made known his skepticism and contempt for the notion of bringing about peace by lying in bed before the cameras in an expensive hotel suite. He wanted to provoke John, and he succeeded when he asked if this would have been John and Yoko's response to Hitler—lie in bed and ask for peace? John lost his temper as Capp belittled his answers and his philosophy — Yoko was also drawn into the argument, shrilly defending John and herself. John got personal, attacking Capp rather than his arguments, and Capp responded smugly. After he left the suite, John and Yoko referred to him as "Al Crap," and the bad vibes from that confrontation stayed in the air for much of the afternoon.

Leary and Lennon were both Libras, and I found myself comparing them, noting how much more skilled and relaxed Leary was in the role of public spokesperson, and thinking that it reflected years of experience, that maybe Leary represented where Lennon would be as a public person and communicator in a few more years. John's weakness was also his charm — that he was an amateur, a sincere and committed fool rushing in where angels might well hesitate. He was slightly over his head dealing with people other than disc jockeys and the pop press — but that was what he wanted, I think. It was the thrill and the vulnerability and the chance to make a difference in the world that drew him and Yoko into situations that would challenge them, stimulate them, confront them with more than what they already knew they could handle. John Lennon knew as well as anyone in the world in 1969 that great creativity starts with the willingness to take real risks.

If I remember right, we visited John and Yoko on May 31st and June 1st, 1969. The moon was full in Sagittarius. As night fell on the 31st, Derek Taylor closed the suite and ushered everyone out except himself, me, Tim and Rosemary, and John and Yoko. The Lennons got out of bed and we sat in a circle on the carpet, ate dinner, listened to John play some new songs on his acoustic guitar, and then we all just sat around and shared who we were and what was going on in our lives. Derek and I stayed more or less in the background of the conversation as John and Yoko and Tim and Rosemary got to know each other.

Playboy didn't publish the conversation after all, and I no longer have a copy of the tape or the transcript. I remember I called the story, "Things We Said Today." "Someday when we're dreaming, deep in love, not a lot to say, then we will remember..."

Tim and Rosemary talked about the ranch they were living on in southern California—how there were different parts of the ranch at different altitudes, corresponding to states of consciousness, so that when they wanted to go to the highest state they would pack whatever they could carry and climb a mountain on or near the property, and camp out for days on a high mesa, taking acid, communing with the universe.

John and Yoko responded enthusiastically with stories of an island they visited in Scotland, and a cruise to Greece where, John confided, he slept outside for the first time in his life—in a sleeping bag on the deck of the ship. Looking up at the stars. As a California hippie, I was amazed at his inexperience, his naivete—and moved by his enthusiasm for each new thing he was discovering in the universe. Yoko's voice was small and whispery, and she opened up in our small circle much more and much more gently than earlier in the day, in the public spotlight. The two couples talked enthusiastically about the power of presenting an image to the world that isn't one person, the individual hero, but rather the loving male-female partnership, man and woman working together and supported by each other's love, as the new role model for an evolving world. Tim acknowledged the revolutionary power of John and Yoko's *Two Virgins* album cover portrait – not just that they were naked, but that they were there as man and woman together. John played *Give Peace A Chance* for us, and taught us the song. He talked about the fun he was having songwriting by himself. Tim talked about his campaign for governor of California, and said that the campaign slogan was "Come Together – Join the Party." John offered to contribute a campaign song, and started writing it on the spot. There was a freeness, a spontaneity to his creative energy that gave me a bit of insight into how the Beatles worked their magic. They were caught up in a whirlwind momentum – starting from the night John stamped on the floor in Hamburg in frustration and the crowd started stamping back, a momentum still rising in May of '69 even though the Beatles were already almost a memory – and they had the grace to lean back and be present within the craziness, and let their creative energy draw from and be supported by the energy that was whirling around them. "Here's my new song." Reach out, grab a melody, tell the truth about what seems to be happening in the moment.

There was a lot of magic in that hotel room that evening, having nothing to do with fame or great plans but just person to person, the space of the moment, heart to heart. As much was shared in the silences as in the talking or the music.

The next day the circus went on around John and Yoko's bed, as before. And at some point late in the morning we all got hustled off to a room somewhere else in the hotel and served as an impromptu chorus on John Lennon's first solo single (credited to "Plastic

Ono Band"). It was fun. John and Yoko were playing together, doing the unexpected, riding the wild tide of the times and of their particular role in the eye of the storm, spontaneously, naively, courageously, egotistically and good-naturedly turning it into theater, music, politics, art. They flew back to London the next day. Tim and Rosemary and I hitched a ride on the six-seater plane hired by CBC to get Al Capp back to Boston, and when the plane stopped in Vermont to refuel I decided to go visit a girl I knew at Bennington. I saw the Learys again, but not together; and that was the first and last time I ever met John and Yoko.

That was 1969, a good year for great adventures. Now it's 1986, and I'm reading in *Rolling Stone* that U2 and Sting and others are going to do a six-city benefit tour for human rights in June, culminating in a huge show at Giants Stadium, and I'm scheming about how to get invited along for the ride...

Musicians showed up at Live Aid for the same reasons that I woke up at dawn and got on the bus for the *March on the Pentagon*... they respected the cause *and* they didn't want to miss out on the action. We are attracted by the feeling that something important is happening and that we can be a part of it, or at least be there as it happens. This is a major consideration in rock concert attendance — everybody's talking about the ZZ Top show next weekend, anticipation is building, this is going to be something really big, are you going to miss it? It may seem inappropriate to compare cruising down to the Cow Palace to see Rush or Motley Crüe — one show on a 90-city tour — with the spirit that brought Woodstock together, but in fact it's the same thing. The buzz that brought me and 399,999 other people to

Woodstock was the same buzz that runs through the high school locker room days before a big heavy metal show — this is the hot one, everybody's going, outrageous music, a wild time, be there or be square. Timing is everything. When enough energy flocks together in one place at one time, for better or worse, you make history... and often the hunch that this could become history (even very local, short-term, transient history) is a factor in bringing the energy together.

And it doesn't just apply to rock festivals or big shows. Among other things, it also applies to whether the magic is or isn't there in a new single by Prince or the Rolling Stones. It's exciting to see a wave rising and jump on it before it crests. And kind of a bummer if it fizzles out, but as long as there are some big ones now and then — occasional miracles — we'll probably keep coming back for more.

I need a miracle every day, but I settle, not always happily, for what I can get.

The thing that most surprises me about rock videos is I find myself seeing a video once and remembering the song. I don't mean I remember that that's the song with the video of the horse wearing pantyhose; I mean I remember the tune and some of the words, which almost never happens the first time I hear a song on the radio (or on a record). This could be because I'm paying more attention to the video, but my experience is that it's hard to remember (form a gestalt of) most songs the first time I hear them even if I give them my full attention. But I do seem able to quickly form a gestalt, and one that exists apart from the visual, when I am exposed to a song in video rather than purely audio form.

What I suspect is that the song in video form actually reaches me in a different way, because of the mixed media; I take it in differently, and it is received and processed differently in my mind. Visual/musical does not equal visual plus musical. The two media get together and produce a third animal, one that's been evolving slowly for quite a while but that may start evolving very quickly, and startlingly, in the new visual/musical environment.

The best analogy I know of for what I'm talking about is the relationship between music and words in songs. The impact of a song is quite different from the impact of a tune plus the impact of a poem. A music video is potentially as distinct from a song as a form of human communication as a song is distinct from a poem (or a melody). Perhaps this is obvious, but it seems to me quite striking. The relative banality of most of what appears on MTV should not blind us to the fact that rock and roll has exploded into a whole new realm, a realm with all the space and creative potential of rock's existing formats, which are the single, the album, and the live performance.

But (I'm thinking out loud here) is video really tied to rock in an essential way, or is it just a historical accident that music video has emerged as a popular and influential form as an extension of rock and roll's current popularity? Perhaps some other form of music, past or future, will turn out to fit more meaningfully with the video form, and rock videos will become a thing of the past or a secondary genre as the mainstream heads off in some other direction.

Rock and roll won't necessarily live forever, you know. Perhaps future historians will look back and say that the turning point, the beginning of its fall from grace after a long period of dominance, was its failure to adapt commercially and creatively to the real possibilities inherent in the marriage of music, words, and moving images.

Which brings us back to an early and stubborn question: what do you mean, what do we mean, what do I mean by "rock and roll"? What gives it its distinct identity? Does it still have one?

It is interesting to speculate on the role John Lennon's early death may have played in reaffirming (or anyway prolonging) rock's dominance. I say this because I don't see the Beatles, the most popular musical act of the modern era, as inevitably and always being perceived in the public eye as rock and roll musicians. (True, they *were* rock and roll musicians, but that doesn't always count for much. Does the public think of Jesus as a Jew?) It is not hard for me to imagine a future history in which the Beatles were actually rock and roll musicians who moved past that early in their careers to become the harbingers of the new world music, --- ---, a music whose nature I won't try to speculate on except that it might be much more pop and not in any significant way connected to what I would call rock or rock and roll.

In a sense didn't this happen before? Didn't Elvis become much more of a ballad singer, a pop figure, than a rocker? Yes, but because of the resurgence of rock in the 1960s, people's memories of him as the original rocker kept that image of him alive. His influence as a rocker was much greater than his influence as a pop singer, even though he was the latter for many more years, and so it is as a rocker that we remember him. But only, I think, because rock stayed around and out-

But only, I think, because rock stayed around and out-lived him; if pop in its schmaltzier forms had really taken over, he'd be remembered today as the great pop vocalist.

The jury is still out on the Beatles, but there can be little question, in 1986 at least, that the image of the Beatles that has survived is much more the John Lennon version than the Paul McCartney version. The reason for this is John's martyrdom, I think; a month before Lennon died McCartney was really by far the more popular and better known of the two. But the assassin's bullet guaranteed, perhaps forever, that the spirit of John Lennon would be, to the public, the spirit of the Beatles.

And of the Beatles, it was John alone who stood squarely in the public eye for the musical and personal values that I anyway associate with rock and roll. Per-haps this is unfair—wasn't it Paul who sang all that great Little Richard stuff? Wasn't it John who went off totally into avant garde pretension at a time when the others might have been ready to return to their roots? Yeah, quite possibly. But when we're talking myth and legend, things are what they appear to be. And with John Lennon's death, the Beatles appear in retrospect much more closely associated with the concept "rock and roll" than they would likely be if he were still among us (watching wheels and singing "grow old along with me").

"It's better to burn out/than it is to rust," Neil Young sang in his ballad for Johnny Rotten ("hey hey, my my/rock and roll will never die"). Then old Neil turned around, stuck out his tongue, put on a Reagan button and began publicly rusting in the most flagrant manner. He always was an ornery one.

Anyway, burning out rather than rusting, especially in the form of dying young (Lennon made it just in time; he'd turned forty a few months earlier), is definitely central to the spirit of rock and roll. I'm not saying this is a good thing; I'm just acknowledging that it is one of the cornerstones of the rock aesthetic. Even today Pete Townshend often seems to wish he *had* died before he got old, which may be more pathetic than heroic but it does show how hard it is to stop saluting old flags. And anyway, the primary issue here is not dying young and leaving a handsome corpse. The primary issue is being *willing* to die— which means, willing to risk it all to create something real right now. Kick out the jams. I don't know if the Rolling Stones still stand for that, but people think they do, and that gives them their value as icons. I don't know if John Lennon stood for that at the end (yes I do—listen to *Walking on Thin Ice*), but he does now, in people's minds and hearts (including mine), and as a result so do the Beatles, and perhaps this in some small way has something to do with why rock and roll today as far as I can tell is as alive and lively as ever.

Psychocandy I'm not sure about yet—it kind of plateaued out just when I thought it would blow me away, but it still could turn out to be wonderful and I'll definitely keep playing it—but in the meantime Elvis Costello or Declan MacManus as he may prefer to be called is turning out to be miracle enough for the whole week. Three or four listens into *King of America* I'm thinking that this could belong in a category with *Blood on the Tracks*, a category that previously had only one album, and one artist, in it. Is this possible? Probably not, but ask me next week. Anyway I'm pretty pleased with how that trip to Tower Records worked out. I guess it's worth suffering through information overload if you can manage to get in and get out with the goods in spite of the hostile fire.

Next step for me is to check out MTV for a while, and rent a few videotapes. This presents some problems, since I have no TV, no cable, no VCR, but I think the neighbors can help.

Rock music is everywhere in the 1980s. And it's not just the top 40. Every third male teenager I see is wearing a Rush t-shirt. Bumper stickers for hard rock radio stations blossom on cars whose owners are clearly past 35. Is this good? Not necessarily. But it's not necessarily bad. Just like we fantasized many years ago, rock music is becoming a universal language (splintered into thousands of local dialects, of course). And I don't just mean universal like we're all eating the same McDonalds-burgers and drinking the same crummy beer and listening to the same generic movie theme songs. I mean universal language like we can and do actually use it to communicate our individuality to each other, to affirm and explore and strengthen our interconnectedness.

What is this rock and roll stuff? Mostly my method for answering that question is to point at it when I see it. If your reaction is to look away in order not to be burdened with more information, believe me I understand completely.

Chapter Seven

"The night/is young/and full of possibilities..."
— Anita Ward

I don't think I've lost track of what I was searching for
when I began this adventure, but I could be wrong
about that. It's funny how you start out looking for the
truth about the most mysterious and all-encompassing
creative form of our times, and end up giving advice to
record companies and consumers on where to invest
their bucks. "Quick, over here, this is hot, this will be
the next big thing!" Music biz is like the stock market:
get in, get out. One day you're a hero, another day
you're a goat. You can't make money following the
crowd or ignoring them; you have to run where they're
running, just a little bit ahead of them. Do that long
enough, and people will think you're a leader. Worse,
you might even think so yourself.

It's hard for me to remember that I don't have to be
in touch with what's happening. All I have to do, to be

true to the spirit of rock and roll, is have a good time while I'm consuming the stuff.

What's the purpose of a map, then? Well, I'd say one thing is to give us the courage to get off the interstate, and explore the countryside; and another thing is to help us find our way back to the interstate sometimes. It's like the secret of the universe is being able to separate and unite. Or you could say the greatness of rock and roll lies in its eclecticism, and in its universality. When you're on the mainline, rock opens the door to a million possibilities; when you're lost out there in the possibilities, rock's solid backbeat can bring you back to the mainline again.

Mainline doesn't necessarily mean mainstream. Last night was the annual Bay Area Music Awards Show in San Francisco. The readers of *BAM* magazine vote on the "bests" of the previous year, and the show is an Oscars-type awards ceremony with a variety of live performances — a benefit to raise money for the Bay Area Music Archives. Anyway, Huey Lewis was voted Bay Area Musician of the Year for the third year in a row, and he and his band copped the award for Outstanding Group, again for the third straight year. I didn't go to the show (caught Fishbone at the Stone instead), but I went to one of the parties afterward. Huey jammed on stage with the party band — played harmonica and did a little singing on *Lucille* and a generic uptempo blues number. It was fun. Huey Lewis is unquestionably a nice guy. And you can't get much more mainstream (U.S.A. 1985 version) than the soundtrack of Steven Spielberg's cute, enjoyable, rock 'n' rolly movie *Back to the Future.*

But (no offense) this isn't what keeps rock and roll alive. This isn't the interstate. This is the bypass that used to be the main road, the one with all the motels and gas stations and fast food joints and tourist traps, a piece of the highway we keep around for sentimental reasons and because, although it may not go anywhere, it sure brings in the cash. This is the mainstream. Most of the time, in rock and roll, it's a total dead end – or, to be charitable, a loop.

The mainline is something else. What comes to mind when I use that word is the Velvet Underground's classic 17-minute recording *Sister Ray* (1968), with the repeated phrase "I'm searching for my mainline." The next sentence is "I couldn't hit it sideways," so we can presume that the reference is to shooting drugs, probably heroin. But that's never been what the song is about to me, for all the seventeen years that I've been in love with and fascinated by this piece of music. What it's about is a kind of centrality, like a purpose in life around which everything else can be organized. I'm simplifying. *Sister Ray* is about a feeling. A big feeling. I can't tell you the name of the feeling, or otherwise describe it, but I know I've felt it many times.

I'm not alone. The showcase song on Mojo Nixon's first album, *I Saw Jesus at McDonald's,* is actually a remake of *Sister Ray* and Mojo acknowledges this as he sings it (he combines it with – among other things – Jonathan Richman's *Roadrunner,* another undeniable rock classic which itself owes a lot to *Sister Ray*). *Psychocandy* by the Jesus and Mary Chain is drenched in Velvet Underground influence from the *Sister Ray* period and earlier. Henry Rollins of Black Flag lists *White Light/White Heat* as one of his two favorite albums and refers to *Sister Ray* as "the monster that waits on side two... Play this a few times and the bugs will leave your house and your neighbors will hate you forever." (*Spin*, November 1985)

And so forth. The Velvet Underground sing about "my mainline" and also they *are* mainline, one of the indisputable gold standards backing up the identity, the Platonic essence, of rock and roll. There are others, some of which I feel fairly sure of. Early Chuck Berry, particularly his guitar leads, his lyrics, his attitude (which has never changed, actually – another gold standard – hang up Chuck Berry's and Keith Richard's attitudes on a wall somewhere and you'd definitely have yourself a rock and roll museum), his voice, his walk, his way of holding his guitar. Early Who singles. (Bono starts singing *The Kids Are Alright* during the encore on one of my U2 concert tapes.) The Buddy Holly opus. Dylan's *Like A Rolling Stone*. The Rolling Stones on London Records (U.S.), plus parts of *Exile* (if that's too much, I'll settle for a couple of handfuls of singles plus *12x5, Now, Between the Buttons*, and *Let It Bleed*). The Kinks: *All Day and All Night* and *You Really Got Me*. The Byrds' *Greatest Hits*. Pink Floyd, *The Dark Side of the Moon*. Phil Spector's great sides. The Beach Boys' singles through *Good Vibrations*. Beatles tracks: no easy agreement here – I'll go for the U.K. albums *Please Please Me, Rubber Soul*, and *Sergeant Pepper*, plus *A Hard Day's Night, I Feel Fine, Eight Days A Week, Ticket to Ride, Daytripper, Strawberry Fields,* and *Hey Jude*. Elvis: *Mystery Train* and your choice of a dozen other basic tracks. The Sex Pistols' singles, from *Anarchy in the UK* to *Holidays in the Sun*. Jimi Hendrix's *Are You Experienced?* and assorted other tracks. I should never have started this. Motown: we could begin with the singles chosen for their CD compilations of songs by Smokey Robinson and Holland–Dozier-Holland. Atlantic / Stax-Volt: you couldn't claim their entire *History of Rhythm and Blues* box as a rock and roll gold standard, but certainly you'll find our mainline running through that box on every record. Everly Brothers. James Brown. Neil Young's *Everybody Knows This Is Nowhere*.

The Doors' first album. That last paragraph was a big mistake (lists are a mistake), albeit an instructive one. *Sister Ray* is rare, a single rock track whose traces can be found everywhere. And I mentioned hearing Velvet Underground songs on successive nights from the Beat Farmers and Lone Justice. The Velvets never made it big (not even middle-sized, not even enough-to-pay-the-bills-for-a-few-months) while they were together, but they are arguably the single most identifiable musical influence across the broadest spectrum of rock performers in the '70s and '80s, as Chuck Berry (arguably) was in the '60s. The Doors, on the other hand, made an album that—well here, listen to what the record company says on the back of the CD: "Though the work of other important bands of the late 1960s now seems to be locked squarely in that era, *The Doors* could just as easily have been recorded and released in the 1980s." This is certainly true. The record is timeless, mysteriously so, much more than any single album by the Beatles or the Stones. Another gold standard. But I think you have to look far and hard to find specific Doors influences in today's music...okay, The Cult's singer does an interesting Morrison imitation in some of his videos, but their music doesn't sound Doors-inspired to me. Heavy metal fans and musicians acknowledge Hendrix as a founding father (Sandy Pearlman and I could probably rewrite heavy metal history if we'd swear we saw Jimi Hendrix and Jimmy Page sit down together one of those summer nights in '67 at Brad Pierce's Salvation club under Sheridan Square, and overheard them planning out the next twenty years of guitar rock in minute and accurate detail), but although heavy metal may mirror a lot of Morrison's stances, gestures, and obsessions, he is seldom if ever acknowledged or referred to.

Why not? Why do the Velvets never sell records, but influence everybody, especially musically, and the Doors sell records forever and always seem of the moment yet their music has seldom been quoted by other bands in the near-twenty years since their ascendance? I'm more interested in the question than the answer, and I'm interested in the question because this is the realm I refer to as rock's mainline. It's the way John Lennon's *Revolution* picks up and reworks Buddy Holly's guitar from *Peggy Sue* (illuminating in retrospect how revolutionary, how ahead of his times Holly was as a rock guitarist, demonstrating how rock as we know it today was already understood and being explored back then, by white outsiders as well as r&b geniuses). The place where these questions come from and these observations are made (and argued with, and refuted, whatever) is the place where rock and roll lives, the well from which it continually draws and is nourished. This is Bruce Springsteen with his pin-ups of Ronnie Spector and his copy of *Roy Orbison's Greatest Hits*. This is Maria McKee singing *Fortunate Son*.

When I was in Japan in 1972 I visited Harry Hosono and he played the three Buffalo Springfield albums, which he acknowledged were still among his favorite records. That influence is probably not obvious in his later work with Yellow Magic Orchestra and other fascinating synthesizer/pop/avant garde experimentations, but on the other hand it doesn't seem strange to me that a musician who liked those albums so much would go on to make significant and popular and groundbreaking rock music. He just gave off this aura of being passionately, helplessly, connected to the mainline of rock and roll energy. I remember when I first heard the Buffalo Springfield, trying to pick out the influences on their first album, not for academic reasons but because they kept reminding me of somebody, or various somebodies, and I couldn't quite remember who. Possibly a dream image, someone familiar but who never actually existed, like a hybrid of the Beatles with the Everly Brothers, with a sprinkling of someone slightly less probable, maybe Jimmie Rodgers or Sam Cooke. That's not right, but like that, you see — something I knew I heard before (something I used to love) but I couldn't quite place it, just out of reach of my memory.

(Maybe it was a memory of the future: you know, "This is great, this is like Poco and Crosby Stills and Nash and all of Neil Young's solo albums and the best of the Eagles on a single disc.")

Huey Lewis is pleasant but inconsequential. And that's just fine, I'm not saying that everything in rock music has to be Significant, but on the other hand I think every work of rock music should strive to be at least as pretty and as awesome as Chuck Berry's *Memphis,* even if maybe nothing ever will be again.

John Fogerty's *Centerfield* won the Bammy for 1985 Bay Area Album of the Year. That record has a fantastic sound, it makes you tingle all over, and the title song and *Old Man Down the Road,* are classics, but the rest of the material falls short, falls just this side of the Other Side that Fogerty is so eminently capable of reaching. Translator's third album, with its thin sound and its wimpy studio representation of Dave Scheff's brilliant drumming (this is the record they put out last year, not the one that's about to come out that I've been raving about), was probably a better album than Fogerty's. It starts slow but shows more of itself on each new listening. Fogerty's record sounds best the first time, to my ears, and that's not okay in music we want to live with for all eternity. (Seventeen years with *Sister Ray*! And it still sounds infuckingcredible. I can't believe it.)

¤

Video is a great source of information. I love information, but I also find it oppressive. I can sit and read a new copy of *Billboard* for hours and hours. MTV is terrific, because I'm usually curious about what the current hits are, and MTV not only plays them, it identifies them, at the beginning and the end, whereas with radio these days you wait half an hour to find out what that song was, and then they may or may not remember to tell you. The information-gatherer that I am likes knowing what song this is as I listen to it. And MTV goes further in feeding my curiosity: I can see what sort of costumes Kiss is wearing these days, I can get a visual image of a new group like Mister Mister—both what the people look like, and also what image they're trying to project (i.e., who they think their audience is).

All this is fascinating, but meanwhile the part of me that really loves rock and roll and isn't just curious to find out the latest gossip, chart positions, and styles, gets anxious and restless, because there's very little satisfying music on music television, and damn little in the way of genuinely communicative visual imagery. I've seen fifty or sixty MTV clips in the last couple of days, and while many of them were "interesting" for various reasons, I don't think I saw a single clip that actually moved me. Whitney Houston's *The Greatest Love of All* pulled at my heartstrings a little, but that's different. That's manipulation, not communication.

I did see things that made me angry. Pat Benatar's video for *Le Bel Age* is attractive and makes me think I could like this song, but I'm distracted by the fact that it's a cigarette commercial from start to finish, and of the very worst type — a clip that shows young people how sexy and cool it is to smoke. Then there's Marilyn Martin's *Night Moves,* which is one of these "you never quite know what's going on" mini-melodramas, but after seeing it twice I believe it actually romanticizes serial murder! How 1980s can you get?

And I'm frustrated, because I want to talk about videos that excite me, just as I choose to talk about music that excites me, and I'm not coming up with any candidates. I find it particularly hard to come to terms with the fact that I'm bombarded on music television with images of bands playing music to excited audiences, and virtually every one of these images is phony. The musicians I'm watching are not making the music I'm hearing (except for one ancient clip of Jimi Hendrix at the Monterey Pop Festival). They're pretending to make music. They're playing air guitar.

They're mimes. This used to be called lip-syncing, and we sneered at it then. Now it's much easier to get good live recordings of rock and roll; but marketing considerations force the musicians to go on faking it. These clips are promotional films intended to sell records — if they were shot live the music would sound different than the studio-made record that's being sold. So we get all of the pretense, and damned little of the soul, of rock music.

What I see in broadcast video is a fabulous form, a tremendously exciting medium, that isn't being used yet, that's waiting for its geniuses, its Beatles, its Chuck Berry, its Beach Boys, Stones, or Dylan to come along. Talking Heads deserve some credit for breaking ground in this direction. Is there anyone else? If not, they're coming, I'm sure of it. Someone who will conceive of the music, the words, and the images as a single unit, who will create as freely in this form as Dylan has in words-and-music, as Picasso did in almost every medium he explored.

So after I arranged with my friends to watch MTV and use the VCR at their house, I went over to the video store and rented four tapes: *Scenes from the Big Chair* by Tears for Fears, *Through the Camera's Eye* by Rush, *Under A Blood-Red Sky* by U2, and *Sun City* by Artists United Against Apartheid. After two days I brought them back to the video shop with regret — I want to spend more time with all of them, keep them around the way I keep records around, watch and listen to them some more as the spirit moves me. I'd feel bad about not being able to afford to buy all the videotapes I want, and the equipment to enjoy them at home — except I'm old enough to appreciate how privileged we are to have access to this equipment, this medium, at all. Rock and roll came into existence and has steadily grown in popularity as a response to the increasing variety and decreasing cost of consumer electronic equipment—portable AM radios, to begin with; 45 rpm phonographs; electric guitars; car radios; later, stereo component phonographs at a price any college student could afford; eight-tracks; cassettes; FM portables and car stereos—and the process continues now with VCRs, inexpensive tape dubbing equipment, the Walkman, compact discs, and no end in sight. Rock music has been the beneficiary of this wave of new technology—and it has also spurred it and supported it. The symbiotic relationship between rock and the expanding technology of "home entertainment" is probably worthy of a book in itself.

For my part I'm just delighted that even though I missed Prince's 1985 tour and John Lennon's 1972 performance, I can now get at least a taste of what those shows were like by walking down the street and renting a tape for three or four dollars. This is exciting. It again makes rock and roll an even bigger playground than it has been, it opens up new possibilities for the artists and for the audience. And maybe the very newness of it, the fear of the unknown as well as the fear of disappointment, is what has made me hold back—that live Prince tape has been catching my eye ever since it appeared in the stores, but seven months later I still haven't gotten around to renting it. I don't have the music videotape habit yet. Judging from sales and rental figures, the American public doesn't yet either. But this is going to change, and soon. All it will really take is an original long-form music video as good and as universally irresistible as *A Hard Day's Night*. It's coming.

Last summer, when I was in love with *Shout* by Tears for Fears, I saw the video of the song once and thought it was wonderful. I didn't have much access to MTV at that time, and I remember wanting to see the clip again (for the joy of it, and also wondering if I'd be as impressed by repeat viewings) and not knowing how or when I would. I wished Tears for Fears would put out a videotape of *Shout,* so I could see it on demand (instead of watching TV for hours, hoping it might come on). Well, they finally did, many months after the fact. Apparently the record company strategy is not to release compilations like this until every song on an album that might be released as a single has been — partly so they can control the timing of when clips are aired, and also I suppose because new clips don't get filmed till they see how the last song (and vidclip) did in the marketplace. The result, anyway, is that the video album tends to come out only after the original album has run its course. Yesterday's papers.

In the future, perhaps, everything will be digital, and we'll be able to order videos of individual songs, which will be instantly transferred over phone lines to our combination personal computer/music disc/video disc player (and billed to our credit accounts at the same time). There will be a broadcast service, so we can be exposed to new product in the first place, but they'll figure out some way that you can't copy it for replay without being charged for it. And in addition to the general public broadcast (radio station/TV station type), you'll also be able to order up promotional previews of anything that's for sale — dial up an index for "new releases, punk/new wave/ minimalist" and then enter the code numbers for each song or album or video or video album you want to preview.

Until then it's still necessary to actually move your physical body to the video shop, and maybe breathe some fresh air on the way. The Tears for Fears tape is a compilation of seven live performances and five music television clips (called "conceptual" to distinguish them from the live clips), with interview material and scenes of them setting up various live broadcasts and video shoots. It's a hodgepodge, predictably, but (surprisingly for this group) a modest one, not attempting to do more than give a casual look at the people in the group and tell a few of the stories behind the songs.

What I came away with: the *Head Over Heels* video is just as awful as I thought it was when I saw it on TV (and a look behind the scenes at how the video was made doesn't help). The *Shout* video is not as great as I first thought, and parts of it are quite predictable, but it does a good job of representing the song, can be seen again and again I think, and for some reason the brief bit with the bass-player's fingers during the bass-dominated bridge is quite wonderful, here at least there is a kind of transcendence. All the other images, the ocean and the sky and the children and people walking downstairs, are brought together and given a power because of this moment, the walking drumsticks and especially the fingers on the bass, when the video really becomes the music, reaches beyond itself. The faces of the singers at the beginning, and the timing of the camera pan, the way they're facing in different directions, also sets the video up with a greater charge, a dignity and excitement that carries over and uplifts much of the more banal or ordinary footage. Their other hit video, *Everybody Wants to Rule the World,* is, like the song, both calculated and inspired – the images of the ultralight plane and of people on their holidays really project the mysterious lightness of the song, the quietly-contained confidence and joy that give it its power. And both *Shout* and *Everybody* succeed by using images without tying them to a story line.

The live stuff is unimpressive, partly because it's so broken up by interview material that it can't build on itself, it's a series of unrelated moments rather than a concert. Tears for Fears do have a tape that's all live material, and I'd like to see it, although the material on this tape suggests that their live performance is not much more than a good arena representation of their recordings. I like the moments when one of the horn players dominates the video and the audio – their personalities jump through for some reason, more than the singers' even. The main effect of the interview material for me was to remind me on the one hand that Ian Stanley and Manny Elias contribute a lot to the sound and identity of the group, despite the fact that pictures of Tears tend to concentrate on the two singers...and on the other hand, that it's Roland Orzabal who dominates the group in terms of writing almost all the material (and doing most of the talking on this tape), whereas again the visual image their covers and publicity presents had me thinking of Roland and Curt Smith as equal co-creators. And I find I like Roland as he comes across here somewhat more than I expected to – he may be a twit but he's a likeable one, not at all the insufferable package of pretension that Sting is in his movie or Mark Knopfler is in his interviews.

I wouldn't watch *Scenes from the Big Chair* a lot or recommend it highly, but it has some good moments and does add to my enjoyment of Tears for Fears' recordings. I come away from it more optimistic about their ability to make good records in the future — I'd been skeptical because *Songs from the Big Chair*, in spite of *Shout*, was such a step down into ambition and confusion from the elegance and power of their lovely first album *The Hurting*. I'd figured international superstardom would deliver the *coup de grace*, but after seeing this tape I have more confidence in Roland Orzabal's ability to shrug off the distortions of success and attention and go on writing great songs.

I rented the Rush tape as part of a continuing effort on my part to open my own musical horizons. This started with a woman in the midwest who found out about my book project and has been sending me tapes, letters and clippings to call my attention to those aspects of rock that mean the most to her. She's in her mid-thirties, a combination hippie/born-again Christian/heavy metal fan (no, she's not into Stryper — she likes Kiss and Motley Crüe and the Scorpions, the crude stuff) who also loves Kansas, the Doors (discovered them in the late 1970s, as did hundreds of thousands of other new Doors fans, even though their last album came out in 1971), Supertramp, Led Zeppelin and, most of all, Rush. Out of respect for her enthusiasm, I arranged to see Rush when they came to the Bay Area a couple of months ago.

Unfortunately, I decided to go with a friend of mine who's a well-known local rock writer. Halfway through the show he and another friend decided they couldn't take any more, and we retired to a bar in the upper rear of the arena, from which you could see the show but not really hear it (we were behind glass). He disliked what he was hearing; I couldn't say I was enjoying it, but I was very impressed by the audience's enthusiasm (not typical unthinking heavy metal enthusiasm; this was about the music, the quality of the performance — somehow I could tell) and I wanted to stay with it and see if it would start making sense to me. I wasn't willing to be a pill about it, however, and besides we'd come in the same car. So my exploration into the Rush concert experience ended prematurely.

I probably wouldn't have gained much from staying for the whole show. The music was *very* loud, as it is at all heavy metal shows (Rush used to be a heavy metal band, but is no longer regarded as such, having gone off in a "progressive" direction all its own). At that volume it's impossible to hear lyrics or even melodies unless you're already familiar with the material. So the best way I had of getting a sense of what was happening was to watch the audience. They were young, but there was a wider age range and a much wider social range than at metal shows I've been to, and they were not "partying" — they were hanging on every note of the music, digging it, loving it. My impression was that, as high as their expectations were, the crowd seemed to be getting everything they came for, and more. I came away with a very good impression of the group's musicianship and of their commitment to both their music and their audience.

So I've been listening to some of the Rush tapes that Bobbie sent me, and I'm starting to respond to them. My hope was that watching their video compilation (*Through the Camera's Eye* is music TV stuff from their '82 and '84 albums) would help speed up the process, and it has. I only had time to watch the tape once, and already I'm picking out lyrics and themes and melody hooks from their album *Grace Under Pressure* where it was just a pleasant-sounding noise to me before (anxious and thundering and claustrophobic, but pleasant-sounding). And the more I'm exposed to Rush, the more I respect them. They're doing serious, creative work, both lyrically and musically, in a form (album-oriented-rock, youth division) that has mostly lent itself to endless repetition, self-importance, and grandstanding.

The videos included on the tape are well-made, and if anything are more claustrophobic and political (lots of stuff about nuclear war and conformity and red-baiting) than the songs themselves. *Distant Early Warning,* for example, features a child joyfully straddling a nuclear missile, riding a long trajectory around the globe, intercut with shots of the band performing the song in particularly urgent fashion. It's a powerful and eye-catching bit of film, but I doubt I'd want to see it more than four or five times at the most, whereas the song is something I can listen to again and again. There are aspects of the song not even hinted at in the video — it's a love song, for one thing — that give it a life and power far beyond the limited reach of the video's well-executed imagery and story-line. In general, I'd call these extremely good promotional videos, and a good introduction, as in my case, to Rush and their music and concerns. But the music has a lasting and growing quality that the videos lack. The video clips promote, but after the first few viewings they won't deliver on their own. This is true of the vast majority of

clips made for music TV, and is a major limitation of
the form.

U2's *Under a Blood-Red Sky* is something else. This is
a concert film, made for videotape release, and it's
wonderful. Donna points out that it offers something
you might not get even if you were at an actual U2 concert, which is the opportunity to see close-up the
onstage interaction between the members of the band,
and particularly between Bono and The Edge. The
closeness of the partnership between the singer and the
guitar player, the way they support each other and in-
teract off each other and fill in, as it were, gaps in each
other's personalities, is revealed not through interviews
but in the best possible way, by allowing us to watch
them work together. We also get a magnificent close-in
look at the relationship between Bono and his
audience. And we get great live performances of a
dozen U2 songs, selected from a June 1983 outdoor
concert at Red Rocks amphitheatre near Denver,
Colorado. The setting — rain, the rocks, fires burning in
the middle distance — is wonderfully dramatic, very
suited to U2's aesthetic. This isn't necessarily the perfect representation of U2 in concert, and I'd rather
there were dozens of tapes like this on the market instead of one, but it is a tape I could watch and listen to
over and over again. This is rock and roll extended into
a new medium — different from the concert, different
from the record, different from the live recording, and
just as legitimate and powerful as those other forms can
be. This makes the survival of rock and roll into the
1980s worthwhile.

So does *Sun City*. This is a beautiful example of a
work of rock and roll that is only marginally

mainstream (the *Sun City* single barely made the top 40, while 1985's other cause-oriented records, *We Are The World* and *That's What Friends Are For,* were both number one hits) but that stands as the essence of rock's mainline, its enduring and constantly evolving cultural and musical identity. This is a revolutionary record. The video too is an amazing piece of work — this is one case where I think the video is as strong as the musical recording it's based on, and can stand up to repeated playings as well or better than the record.

Unlike its predecessors, *Sun City* is not a benefit record — it doesn't exist to make money, although all services have been donated and all proceeds go to a nonprofit fund. The purpose of this record is to make a statement, or actually a number of statements, including a musical statement that can never be fully translated into words on paper. The basic statement is "I (we) ain't gonna play Sun City" — a pledge by musicians not to perform in this South African resort complex located in a supposedly independent black state that is in fact a prison for the enslaved. The personal nature of this pledge is part of what makes the song so powerful — it's more than a posture, it's a decision, a commitment, an action.

And then, of course, the song and the record and video are a statement against apartheid, and a seductive but also forceful, no bullshit demand for attention to what is happening in South Africa and how important it is to all of us. The record exists to raise consciousness, increase awareness, focus attention — and it has succeeded.

The song and the video make a further statement by bringing together musical and cultural forces that have never really been allied before. Towards the end of the video co-producers Arthur Baker and Little Steven make reference to this, claiming that very few people listening to the *Sun City* album will have been directly exposed to all of the types of music represented here — represented not in a subjugated, collaborative, me-too context but in all their raw power: rap music and hip hop, contemporary cutting-edge jazz and fusion, the experimental art-rock tradition represented by Peter Gabriel, popular rock and roll as represented by Bruce Springsteen, Clarence Clemons, Ringo Starr, Pete Townshend, Pat Benatar, Keith Richards, U2's Bono, and so forth. When Miles Davis, for one, totally throws himself into a project, you know this is not lip service towards a good cause. This is for keeps. This is war, this is total creative mobilization, for real, for this moment. Somewhere on the videotape Little Steven speaks of the Malopoets who are willing to risk death to be on this record, and it doesn't seem like grandstanding or an exaggeration.

Technically, this work makes use of and pushes the limits of contemporary recording and editing technology in a manner that boggles the mind. It only really began to hit me as I watched the video, and realized that the two versions of *Sun City* and related tracks were recorded not by a large group of stars gathered in a studio, but by 52 performers working alone or in twos or threes in scores of separate sessions in fifteen different studios in New York, London, Los Angeles, Dublin... cobbled together with the same crude and brilliant art that has grown out of "scratching" by club deejays and breakdancers with boomboxes, finding ways to cut into recorded music and extend it and recreate it by adding in patches of noise, huge pounding beats, a cross between the most basic street improvisation and the cutting-edge technology of computer-sampled sound and drum machines and 72-track studios. This is not just the latest manifestation of black pop or studio smarts; this is a new aesthetic, a new way of relating to sound and beat and the power of the human voice, a black/urban/technological folk music/folk poetry that has roots here and roots there but as a whole was never even dreamed of before the last few years.

And *Sun City,* musically closer to a rap record than rock and roll, also exemplifies what rock has always done best: creating a heterogenous unity out of musical and social forces that seem incompatible, hitting and running and disappearing into the night but leaving behind an indelible imprint. Example: the Byrds in 1965 bringing Bob Dylan and the hit parade together with *Mr. Tambourine Man,* achieving this with a gorgeous twelve-string guitar sound that had nothing to do with either Dylan or 1965 pop, yet somehow served perfectly to unite the two. Rock and roll sometimes seems not so much a music itself as a place where extraordinary music happens, and happens very publicly. And then after it happens, rock and roll almost unconsciously redefines itself to incorporate the fait accompli, and then we have "folk-rock" or rap/rock or *Sgt. Pepper* rock or whatever. It's like a snowball that picks up pieces of everything in its path, yet goes on having the same essential characteristics: round, sticky, cold, etc.

The impact of *Sun City* — as a political statement, as a work of spontaneous conceptual art, and as a musical coming-together—will be felt in rock music and in the world, I suspect, for decades to come. It's a door-opener if there ever was one.

And the video, paradoxically, is live and spontaneous even though its genius is in its editing, its intercutting of images and information, its uniting of people singing in different places at different times so it feels like they're singing as one and no phoniness this time, because they really are. What the directors have done is, first, allowed the group energy to lead the process, and, second, edited to the beat of the music, the rhythm of the vision, pointing in the direction of what rock video needs to become — visuals that have a beat, pictures that set the heart dancing. There are places in this video where the suffering of the oppressed and the joy of speaking out come together, where frustration and commitment, confusion and clarity, meet and unite, and what results is movement, a sense of movement that is both sobering and exciting. Are we the world? No one knows for sure — how we feel about who we are changes from moment to moment — but *Sun City* (record and video both) inspires us to risk that possibility.

This is not inconsequential. This is art that matters, not because it's political or topical but because it is so human. It aspires. Rock's willingness to work with the issues of the moment, the technology of the moment, the musical energy of the moment, most of all its willingness to defy authority including commercial and critical authority and to take outrageous risks, to go for spontaneity and edgework rather than calculation and reason-ableness, is the juice that keeps it young, significant, alive.

Most of the records and videos and live shows that fly the flag of rock and roll don't meet these standards, of course. But the ones that do have a lasting impact on everyone who encounters them. They are the mainline. They follow no rules. They make my search worthwhile.

Chapter Eight

"In a dream I was an actor/and I never knew the lines."
— Translator

Conversation, December 5, 1985, with Steve Barton, singer/guitarist/songwriter, member of Translator, and Dave Scheff, drummer, member of Translator.

Steve: "I don't know if I could say what rock and roll is to me, but... Especially being in a group that has a record contract and is about to make a fourth lp — we've seen some real peaks and some real valleys, ups and downs and every other direction, sometimes all at once — but for the most part it's been a pretty positive trip, just because ultimately it's the music that's keeping it together. If it were anything else I think we would have been apart long ago, because the business world is so absurd that if you didn't like the music your band is playing then there wouldn't be any point."

Dave: "So many of the things that we've gone through are because of the dichotomy between what we really want to do and what we're allowed to do, or what we end up doing because of the pressures we think we're under which we might not even be under, trying to second-guess the record business and all that stuff... That's where all the pressure comes in. If you're going to just go do Animotion, you can just do that – it's like a corporate sort of rock band, and I don't doubt that they've played together in clubs for years and years, but then they decided, 'This is what's happening right now, let's design something for that.' "

Steve: "With that in mind, because we have definitely made some attempts to have chart success, like cutting records that we thought would be popular on the charts – one of the most deadly mistakes a recording artist can make, I think – coming through all that, and getting ready to make this new album, in a weird sort of way I feel more focused now. Like today at our rehearsal, one song we did was one I wrote called *These Old Days.* We've been doing some shows lately, and they've been great, but *These Old Days* was an example in my head of a song that had gotten away from at least me, and I knew that was affecting the way it was coming across. I knew I was approaching it differently, and I couldn't put my finger on it. And today we played it, and for some reason things just went [he slaps his hands together], just meshed."

Dave: "Hadn't you guys [i.e., the other members of the band] talked about this?"

Steve: "Not really."

Dave: "Oh, I see. I thought you had all..."

Steve: "I may have said, you know, 'That song's been a little strange for me,' I may have mentioned something, but –"

Dave: "Oh, I thought you'd actually talked about it and decided, uh, 'So the next time we play I'm going to – ' "
Steve: "No. Uh uh. Not at all."
Dave: "Oh, okay. I misunderstood that today. That's why I said, 'You should have said something to me before we played it, I would have done that too.' "
Steve: "Right. No, it was just – That song in particular was one in my own head that – personally one of my favorites that we do, and when it works, should be a very moving and, it should give you chills, really, when it works. And it did today. Because I found I wasn't overplaying it and expecting it – 'Oh, here's the part where it builds up,' 'Oh, now I've gotta be...' I'd been thinking too much about it, not just letting it come through me.

"And that as an example... I oddly feel so ready now to make this record. I feel very centered about it, I'm looking forward to it, I'm excited. And why I started talking about this, I was talking about rock and roll and what it means to me. When I think of making a rock and roll record, to me it's a progression from – I think it starts with the Sun sessions, you know, 1956, which was one mike, and it sounds great, to four-track machines, to *Sgt. Pepper* with two four-track machines, and then it builds up to now, where it's, whatever you want – "
Dave: "Too-many-track machines."
Steve: "Yeah. And computers. But I think you can't lose the essence of that purity of, 'Here's the mike, what can *you* do?' You start off with a blank roll of tape. Or a blank floppy disc. And what you put on it is what's gonna be on it. What you don't put on it won't be on it. And that's just reality. To me, rock and roll

records are nothing more and nothing less than that, it all comes down to, what you choose to put on.

"When I think of rock and roll, I think of making records and live shows. I think they're two separate things, yet part of the same whole. I think we used to consciously separate them too much, to the point where we made one record, our second album, which is a good record, I like it, but it didn't sound anything like what we sounded like live. Nothing. We even tried to recreate that record and sound like it live, instead of making the record sound like us in the first place.

"The lesson there, for us — What I've come to, and it's a realization that's almost new for me, for some reason, even though it's kind of obvious, is you take the thing that is the, not necessarily easiest, but the most comfortable — I mean, there's a lot of songs I could bring in, and I have brought in, that are good songs, and we could play them, and they'd be fine, probably. But then there's songs that you go, 'It goes like this,' and bam!, it's like we've been playing it for ten years. It's like we already know it, it's comfortable, Bob's got a harmony part and a guitar line, it's like, 'Whoa, how did that happen?'

"And I've found that most of our songs that seem to last the longest are those songs, and the other ones seem to fade away, because they're [laughs] too much work, in a way."

Paul: "I believe that has something to do with group identity, doesn't it?"

Steve: "I think so. 'Cause you're talking about, in our group, four people, four individual people. Not everyone's gonna like the same thing, not everyone's gonna want the same thing, in a particular song. But, yeah, it comes down to a group effort, to working together, to get to where everybody can be satisfied."

Paul: "I think that, when you said, 'Certain songs can go bam!, and it's like we've been playing it for ten years' — one song isn't necessarily better than another, but it's like, those that go bam! are vehicles to express — "

Dave: "Those are the obvious Translator songs."

Steve: "Exactly."

Dave: "When you talk about, 'What is rock and roll?'... I think what we're gonna do this time is go into the studio and, from our talks about how we're gonna go about this, which is different from the way we've done any of our other records — it's closer to the way we did our first record than either of the other two — is, we're gonna go in the studio and be Translator. And that naturally, at its best, is great rock and roll. Without trying to go, 'Well, what's rock and roll?, let's go do that.' "

Conversation, January 29, 1986, with Phil Lesh, bass player, member of the Grateful Dead.

Paul: "What is it like to be performing rock and roll at — how old are you now?"

Phil: "Forty-six, in a couple of months."

Paul: "I'm sure there was a time when it didn't seem like you'd still be doing this..."

Phil: "Well, that was at the time in my life when I didn't think I'd ever get to be, I didn't even think I'd live to be thirty years old."

Paul: "Right. Me too."

Phil: "I don't think anybody does. It's not that you're gonna die, it's just that you don't think that far ahead. You know, the next woman, the next gig, the next tune... Whatever."

Paul: "And how intense it's been so far, it couldn't possibly go on."

Phil: "Oh, but life isn't like that. It surprises you. Especially when you start thinking it *can't* get any weirder. I've learned not think that—and of course, it happens anyway.

"But the performing is the same for me now as it's always been, once of course I learned how to actually play and not worry too much whether I was gonna fuck up. 'Cause in our band people fuck up all the time and it never seems to make too much difference, you just keep going. That was very convenient. And besides, at the point we were playing the sloppiest, we were playing so loud that half the time you could make a mistake and nobody would really notice it, at least not out in the audience. So it wasn't like you were as naked as being, say, a jazz soloist, or in a string quartet or something like that.

"But the experience of performing, once you get rid of whatever stage fright or, 'Oh my God, what if I,' 'Oh my God, please don't let me fuck up,' and all that, it's probably the most intense kind of experience you can have. The amount of attention that's being paid to you because you're standing up on that stage, with all those lights, and all this incredible sound system, and this instrument which could probably knock the building down if you let it loose... It's very exhilarating, it's a feeling of power, of course, and you have to say to yourself at some point, 'It's just me.' And then you start wondering, 'Well, why are all these people staring at me? I'm just doing this, I'm just playing the bass.'

"Kesey used to call this 'the pyramid of attention.' At the Acid Tests we really tried to defuse that by having something happening over here or over here or even behind you that would sometimes drown out the bands, 'What the fuck was that!?' and people would turn around and not get locked into staring at the band. And ever since about 1966 that's been all there was, was the pyramid of attention. Because that's showbiz, and that's what people really want to see.

"Performing is like being God for a very short time. Even if you fuck up. Because then you say, 'Ah, I'm human.' 'No you're not—keep going! Keep going!' You've got a gig to play, keep playing.

"In our band, we've been playing together for so long, there's a certain togetherness that we have, and it's amazing, it only comes out when it's really just absolutely the right moment, and the rest of the time we just play along. And we can sound very good even when we're just playing along. And then something just starts happening, somebody plays something that seems right, you know, and we're off!

"That's the only reason I'm still doing it, is because that still happens. In other words, 'I don't know where we're gonna go from this.' If I as a musician had to play our greatest hits on tour, or just do an album tour, like bands do, I don't think I could still be performing, after twenty years.

"It wouldn't be worth my while. The money would be good, and of course it still is, but...

"Thankfully our band still has that ability, even though it may not surface for quite some time in a row...but I've learned to have faith. Besides, it's always interesting. I can always go out and try to play what I, do what I do better than I did the night before. For a long time I didn't have that attitude, and then it came to me that that was a better attitude to have than going out there and saying, 'Well, how shitty is this gonna be tonight?'

"So I started trying to do my best to support what was going on in the band, on individual tunes and stuff, even though I didn't always agree with it. That was a big flash for me, because I'd been one of those guys who always thought I knew where it was at. When you play in a band for twenty years, you find out that everybody knows where it's at most of the time, and you can usually depend on somebody, somebody else in the band to show you something you hadn't thought of.

"That may not make sense in a connective sense, but that's sort of how our band works. We'll be playing along, and all of a sudden I'll realize that I can't hear what Bob's doing, what the fuck is he doing? And I'll be concentrating on him to the exclusion of everything else, and I'll realize that the reason I can't hear him is because he's been doing something that's so complementary—that is to say, opposite but meaningful—to what the rest of us have been doing, that it's like, it's a whole other dimension that I wasn't aware of, and I say, [snaps fingers], and away we go. Or at least, there's a chance.

"For one thing, the volumes at which we play, and the size of the stage, with two drummers and the spacing of the speakers and so on, it's pretty difficult. We even have lag times. If you're ten feet away from someone, and he plays a note, it'll take ten milliseconds, or ten thousandths of a second, for that sound to get to you. So we're trying to figure out a way to squeeze our stage set-up together so we can see each other and hear each other better, and not have to have that horrible lag all the time. Because it really forces you to play on a level where really fine response and interaction is almost impossible.

"So we do it on a broad scale, a broad level, now, and it's still satisfying to do that, but it's getting more difficult, because of the volume and the large space. But we're working on it. And the potential still exists, every time we go out on stage, for me, it exists for us to make new music. We don't always do it, but... That's the only reason I'm still playing in the band. Otherwise, rock and roll, the performance of rock and roll, only goes so far. Especially if you have to do the same stuff over and over again, like almost every other band besides the Grateful Dead does, as far as I know.

"Maybe that's the reason why bands just don't last, or they can't stay together and grow, because first of all in the industry you're forced to go too fast. And second of all, you're forced to condense your thought into these songs and onto these albums every so often, by the industry and by your own desire to be successful and have a lifestyle and so on. And then you're locked into playing that music, in that same way, for — It's a marvelous tape loop, in a way.

"The Grateful Dead — we don't put out records really a lot any more, we'll probably have to put out one soon, but we've been, for the last five years we've been doing nothing but touring. It gets really old, I'll tell you. Travelling is the worst."

Paul: "And you do a lot of it."

Phil: "Seventy gigs last year, eighty this year, I think. But still, it's really worth it, because making a record is only, for us it's only a way to pay off a debt, or fulfill a contract. It's never been as meaningful for us."

Paul: "The Grateful Dead obviously is an anomaly (in that they're one of the most popular rock bands in the world, even though they haven't released an album of new material in the last five years; their success is based entirely on their live performances), but to me that makes it the essence of rock and roll. I mean, I think rock and roll is actually made up of those unique things, rather than – "

Phil: "Rather than the mainstream."

Paul: "Yes. And really always has been."

Phil: "Yeah. The freaks."

Paul: "There's nothing quite like Elvis, or the Beatles, or the Velvet Underground, or whatever, you can't actually – "

Phil: "You can't imitate those things."

Paul: "Or put your finger on it, even, what – "

Phil: "No, it's the totality. The whole is greater than the sum of the parts. When we started playing together, there was that immediate synergy, we could all feel it. We couldn't play well enough to really do it, but we could sure feel it. And since we were all musicians – I understand a lot of rock and roll bands start out and some of them aren't even musicians. And yet they become successful, and they actually play good music.

"Which only proves that rock and roll is the people's art, the people's music. And long may it wave as the people's music."

Paul: "I think it's another exception that proves the rule, in terms of the Dead – to be able to come in with some musical background, and – "

Phil: "And still play rock and roll. And also learn from it. Yeah, that's – Rock and roll has no tradition, and that's why it's so exciting. I mean, even jazz has tradition. The blues has tradition. Rock and roll is an extension of the blues as far as I can tell – "

Paul: "The blues and popular black music too."

Phil: "Yeah, whatever they used to call it, race music or r&b or whatever. That's a uniquely American thing. "Rock and roll is something that is going to make as many people musicians as can be musicians. When I was in college, and then later, before I joined the band, I knew no musicians except the ones I'd gone to school with. Now, even casually on the street, I meet people who, if they're not professional musicians, they play, if they can. People even get together and play in bands and they don't necessarily have eyes to 'make it,' they're just doing it because it's either fun or something to do, I mean at least they're not out there in street gangs. They're playing music together, and I always thought that was the message of rock and roll, especially from San Francisco.

"The way it started out there was, 'See these five or six guys up here playing this music? Well, two years ago we couldn't have done this, or we weren't doing this.' Or, 'Can you dig it? We're so fucked up. If we can do this, you can too!' "

Paul: "I think it applies to the audience, too. Anyone can walk into a Grateful Dead concert, or most rock and roll shows, without knowing anything about it, and get into the music. That's something that gets lost with some forms of jazz, and classical music, where you really need to learn the language before you can hear what you're listening to."

Phil: "That's true. The thing about rock and roll being the people's music— If you're playing rock and roll or even listening to rock and roll, you're still better able to hear other kinds of music, like a Bartok string quartet, or even electronic music, real electronic music, like computer music, that's not necessarily tonal or rhythmic in that sense.

"The best thing about rock and roll is that it has made possible a level of popular music that's worldwide, global, and it's going to be the roots for a classical music of the future which we won't believe. I hope I live long enough to hear some of this music."

Conversation, October 13, 1974, with Bruce Springsteen.
Paul: "Who were you into musically then?"
Bruce: "Let me see. In '68, I think I was listening to... Dylan."
Paul: "*John Wesley Harding*."
Bruce: "I never listened to *John Wesley Harding*. I never listened to anything after — I listened to *Bringing It All Back Home, Highway 61, Blonde on Blonde*... That was it. I never — to this day, I haven't heard his earlier albums. And to this day, I have never heard his later albums. It was strange, there was only a short period of time where I related to him. It was only that period where he was really important to me. Where he was giving me what I needed.

"I had never even heard the guy until I heard *Like A Rolling Stone* when it was on the radio, when it was a hit. Because there was no FM airplay at the time, and if there was, not many people had a FM radio. And there were no kids — like '65, I was fifteen — there were no kids at all, fifteen years old, into folk music or anything. There had been a folk boom, but it was generally a college thing. So there was no way of knowing. AM radio was an incredible must in those days.

"The main thing I dug about those albums, the main reason I didn't listen to a lot of his other stuff, is I was never that into folk or acoustic-type music. I dug the *sound*, you know, of what was on those records. Before I listened to anything of what was happening in the song, you heard the chorus and you heard the sound of the band, which was incredible, he had just an incredible sound, and that's what got me.

"I dug the Stones, first few albums, first two, three, four maybe, after that I haven't heard any of their last albums, I've heard the singles, *Tumbling Dice* and stuff, which was great. Same thing with them, like after *December's Children*, and there was *Aftermath*, what else was there? *Between the Buttons*, that's where I started to lose contact with the Stones. What came after *Between the Buttons*?"

Paul: "*Satanic Majesties, Beggars' Banquet, Let It Bleed...*"

Bruce: "Yeah, to this day — See, I never had a record player, for years and years and years. There was a space from where, when I started to live by — when my parents moved out west, from when I was seventeen to when I was twenty-four, I never had a record player. So it was like, I never heard any albums that came out after, like, '67. [laughs] I was never a social person to where I'd go over people's houses and get loaded and listen to records, I never ever did that. I didn't have an FM radio. So I never heard it, I never heard anything. Then I lived with Diane and she had an old, beat-up record player, but only old records sounded good on it, so that's all I played. Play old Fats Domino records, they sound great on it! They sound like trash, they sound terrific.

"A lot of the acts lost what to me was important after that period of time. They just didn't hold it, they just didn't hold— something, they just didn't seem to be able to go further and further. They seemed to have made their statement. Basically the Stones, they make the same statement every record, basically. Without elaborating that much on it.

"I listened to the Yardbirds, Them, the Zombies, all those groups. There was some great stuff on those albums."

Paul: "But mostly, your contact has been through jukebox and AM radio?"

Bruce: "I guess, yeah. I stopped listening to AM radio, too, you know, because it started to get really trashy. And I didn't have a car."

Conversation, December 5, 1985, with Dave Scheff.

Dave: "The drummer is usually perceived as being a hired hand who just keeps the beat. I remember in L.A., we played at the Whisky, and somebody from another prominent L.A. band came up to me and said, 'We're auditioning drummers. Do you like this band that you're in? 'Cause we'd be interested...' I said, 'You don't understand. This is my band.' I couldn't relate to his question. People say, 'So you play for Translator,' as though Translator held these auditions, and everybody went and auditioned, and I got the job so I work for Translator. I say, 'No, I don't play for Translator in the way you mean it. Translator's my band. It's a relationship. I don't work for my wife, I'm married to her.

"It's a weird perception, they see a Keith Moon [of the Who] as an anomaly: 'Yeah, he's the heartbeat of the band, he's really exciting, he really adds a lot.' And that's perceived as unusual. Yet a good rock and roll drummer, that's his function, to be that exciting.

"And anybody who says Ringo Starr wasn't like that should watch the Washington, D.C. film—their first concert in America, before they realized that no one could really hear them anyway, that they didn't have to go for it. 'Cause he was going for it, man, he's, the whole drum set's rocking, hands up like this and he's just smacking the shit out of it. It's amazing, the guy was brilliant, he's a great drummer. I tell all my students, especially this one I've got who's eighteen, he says, 'What should I listen to? I know all the stuff that I grew up with, but what did you grow up with?' And I tell him, 'Check out *She Said She Said,* it's on *Revolver.*' He says, 'Yeah, I think I saw that at the library, I'm gonna check that out tomorrow.' "

Paul: "What drew you in? The Beatles, also?" (Larry, Bob, and Steve had already each told me that they became musicians because of the Beatles.)

Dave: "Yeah. I went and saw the TAMI Show film which was playing with *A Hard Day's Night* when it opened at the Corbin Theatre. I was watching them with my mouth hanging open and a giant smile on my face, just being totally in love with the whole thing and that it was aimed at me. 'Cause I'd listen to the teenagers next door, to the radio station they listened to, and I knew what was going on, but it didn't seem aimed at me. This was the first thing besides maybe the Beach Boys, which was the first record I ever bought, that was really for me, and I was just looking at it just being so in love with the whole thing, and I realized — I don't know what song it was — that I was going [taps out a rhythm] on my knees. And I'm watching, going 'Well, that's the same thing he's doing, and if I can do that, then I can get in a band too, it's even easy, I can already do it.'

"The very next day, this music store, Beechler's Music, was having their grand opening thing, and I went with two friends of mine whose parents were buying them guitars. And they said, 'Yeah, we're going to start a band.' And I said, 'Well, I want to be in it, I want to play drums.' And they said, 'Can you play drums?' I said, 'Yeah.' And they said, 'Well, show us. What if we were to play' and they sang me *Louie, Louie*. And I went over to the high hat, because there weren't any snare drums out, and I went, 'Well I'd go–' [makes sound of drum part for *Louie, Louie*].

"And they said, 'Get some drums and you're in the band.' So I went home and told my parents, 'I need some drums now.' 'Huh? What about Little League?' 'I'm sorry, Little League's over, I need some drums.' "

Conversation, January 29, 1986, with Phil Lesh.

Phil: "Rock and roll is not something you can just pin down and say, 'Okay, it has four chords, and a certain kind of a beat to it, and it either goes like dit-dit-dit-dit or dumm bahh dumm bahh–' But it's not like that. It's a state of mind. So we assumed that it meant, you can do anything you want. As long as you make it comprehensible.

"Which is what all music is all about. Do anything that you want, to do what you want to do, whether you want to express something or just go wheeeee!, have a little fun. And try to make it comprehensible to people by whatever means, whether you use a key, or parallel harmony on the voices, so that people will say, 'Oh! Isn't that sweet.' But at that point, and this was 1965 that I'm talking about, rock and roll was for us a vehicle to make music with, nothing more — our music with. It turned into a lifestyle later on."

Chapter Nine

"Today/I feel like loving you/more than before."
—Jefferson Airplane

"Congratulations," I said to Jack Casady. He was standing in the shadows near the bar in New George's, a club in San Rafael, watching Marty Balin's band come on for their second set of the night. Most of the guys in the band are also members of the Kantner-Balin-Casady Band, which reportedly has just signed a million-dollar deal with Arista Records. Jack screwed up his face, lifted his head slightly and gave me the trademark Casady glare — dour, wry, brotherly, piercing — and muttered, "You know I don't celebrate." I bent my head closer but still caught only pieces of his next few sentences; the gist of it, though, was that there are things to be said, particularly given the political situation now in America and on the planet, and not too many people willing to say them. He seemed to be promising that this new band would make a difference in the world.

Driving home from the club, I turned on the radio and got a string of irresistible oldies: *Hey Jude, Honky Tonk Women, Wooly Bully, Wild Thing.* (Irresistible, anyway, to former '60s-teenagers like myself.) The main reason I listen to music (or talk radio) in the car is that otherwise my mind gets thinking so hard I get distracted from the road. Listening to something keeps me from getting totally lost in my thoughts, but I do still think, and as often happens lately I found myself wondering what it is about these songs that makes them appeal to me.

The common thread seems to be the sound, the attitude, and the beat, and these to me are probably the dominant elements in rock and roll. Lyrics, melody, vocal performance — the elements you might usually think of first when analyzing the appeal of a popular song — are also important, but there's a difference in emphasis. The lyric is the most important variable in the quality and appeal of a country music song. The kind of pop songs we call "standards" rest their appeal primarily on melody. In rock and roll, lyrics and vocal performance often serve primarily to communicate an attitude, and melody is less important than the overall *sound* of a song. "The beat" is generally the most noticeable aspect of the sound, but lots of other elements enter in — "fuzztone" guitar and echo effects on voices are two examples, and there are hundreds more.

Hey Jude certainly has an attractive melody (this can't be said for the other three oldies I heard). But what makes the song great is its sound, and the attitude the sound conveys: calmness, caring, a sense of profound reassurance, escalating to joy. The structure of the song is remarkable; and it's worth noting that structural innovation is a significant subtheme in the history of rock and roll. It is a music in which song structure matters; experiments in structure are encouraged and, when successful, rewarded. This has played a big part in keeping the music young and fresh (over an extended period of time; of course at any given moment any branch of rock is quite likely to be totally mired in its own traditions and self-concepts, structural and otherwise).

What I love most in *Hey Jude* are the screams — the great transitional scream, and then the stuff during the chorus. Here is rock at its most Apollonian and Dionysian both at once, chaos within structure, hysteria within serenity. It's ecstatic. It makes me think that I actually underrated the Beatles during their era, if such a thing is possible. This is the sort of performance and recording that gives rock and roll a reason for existence. Perhaps in the future there'll be another musical environment within which something like *Hey Jude* could be created, but right now rock is the only place where this could have or still could happen.

Honky Tonk Women. The sound. What an incredible sound! From the cowbell that starts it to the crescendo at the end, every note of the vocal, every beat of the drum and thud of the bass, and especially every crunch and ring of the guitars is absolutely gorgeous. All the message is in the sound. The lyrics just serve to prop up and give color to the extraordinary musical and attitudinal environment the sound creates. This is an expression of pure feeling. And again, you couldn't start off with the rules and considerations of any other form of music and create this particular work of genius — not jazz, or classical, or standard pop, or country (as country-flavored as the song is), or folk. Only blues comes close, but you still can't get here from there. To get from blues (or country folk or anything else) to *Honky Tonk Women,* you'd have to invent rock and roll first.

Wooly Bully is the least of these songs — fun to hear again for nostalgic reasons, just as it was fun when it first came on the airwaves (and a great drag after it became a big hit and was played to death). Again, sound and attitude is all there is to this recording, and it does go to show how gloriously eclectic rock (in this case the pop side of rock) can be. Anything can be grabbed up, given a beat and a hook, an appropriately ironic attitude or whatever, and served up as a hit single. And even though record and group may fade into well-earned oblivion after their moment in the sun (Sam the Sham actually had another chart-topping novelty hit the following summer, the atrocious *Little Red Riding Hood*), God only knows what influences sink in to the collective unconscious from stuff like this. Somewhere in the northern plains of Canada some garage band may be at this moment reinventing the Tex-Mex brass boogie sound based on little more than (long-forgotten) exposure to and fascination with *Wooly Bully* at an early age. The process does work like that.

Wild Thing wasted no time in becoming a rock classic — less than a year after the Troggs' single hit number one, Jimi Hendrix was covering it as part of his basic thirty-minute set at his first shows and club appearances in the States — usually as the climax of the set, after *Purple Haze, The Wind Cries Mary,* and *Like A Rolling Stone,* if I remember right. Melodically and rhythmically it's a "version" of *Louie, Louie,* which of course is as pure an example of mainline rock and roll as there is. The genius of *Wild Thing* is the way it slows down the beat and, instead of losing it, manages to make it twice as powerful. This changed rock and roll history; the ramifications of this trick are still being explored by punk and new wave and heavy metal musicians today. Along with this, the vocal is a fascinating combination of passion and restraint: the less feeling the singer (Presley of the Troggs or Hendrix or whoever) puts into the lyrics, the more sexual excitement and power is communicated. The song, totally corny if you just read the lyrics ("groovy" was a dumb word even in 1966), comes across as the essence of cool, a direct descendant of, for example, Carl Perkins's and Elvis's *Blue Suede Shoes*. But louder. Cruder. This is the sound and the attitude a lot of us are looking for when we listen to rock music; and we love it when we find it. *Wild Thing* could even be *about* rock: "Wild thing, think you move me/but I want to know for sure./Come on, sock it to me./[pause]/You move me."

It's been bothering me that there are so many songs and album titles on the charts — and more coming out every day — containing the words "U.S.A." or "America." Seems like cheap exploitation of the phony patriotism that's so sickeningly rampant in this second term of Reagan's kingship. (Lao-tsu said, "When love of country is lost, then people talk of patriotism." I'm sure Marcos in the Philippines talked of patriotism all the time while he was systematically looting his country of an astonishing percentage of its liquid wealth. If he loved his country *at all* could he have robbed it so heartlessly?)

Suddenly, after being stuck in this position for quite some time, I see another possibility. I mean a third possibility—not the obvious alternate that I have been rejecting and still reject, which is that it's perfectly appropriate to be proud of the U.S.A. at this moment in history, perfectly natural and even exciting that we're rediscovering our love for our country and expressing that love in our songs.

The choices I thought I had, the two possibilities, were: a) that all this "what a wonderful country America is" stuff is sincere and I'm just too stuck in my old antiwar '60s mentality to appreciate it; or b) it's a bunch of insincere jingoistic crap and rock music is now helping to sugarcoat injustice and lead us down the path to the next war.

The breakthrough I'm experiencing, the third possibility, came in the form of noticing that while there are five singles in the current top 40 that use our nation's name in their titles (*R.O.C.K. in the U.S.A.*, Mellencamp; *Calling America,* Electric Light Orchestra; *American Storm,* Bob Seger; *For America,* Jackson Browne; and *Living in America,* James Brown), there are only two entries on the album charts that do this, and while one of course is Bruce Springsteen's *Born in the U.S.A.*, which certainly would seem to have set the whole trend in motion, the other is Elvis Costello's new album, *King of America,* the subject of which is self-examination (specifically in the area of man/woman relationships; even more specifically, the aspects of those relationships that have to do with pretense and honesty, desire and fear, security and freedom). Suddenly something went click—don't ask me how this works, I don't know—and I found myself for the first time considering the rather obvious notion that "America" may be showing up a lot in this year's music because it's time for us (not just Americans but the whole world, or at least the "developed" parts of the western world, the primary rock audience) to examine our ideas and (especially) our feelings about "America." It finally occurred to me that this doesn't have to be a good thing or a bad thing, regardless of the impressions I may get from the content of the songs or people's reactions to them. It could simply be seen as a process that's happening, something we need to go through collectively, something that's just naturally going to work itself out at least partly through rock and roll. Personal/collective. Each of us feels our feelings and goes through our own process about this, and somewhere along the line a collective shift takes place. It's already started. The music stimulates it and reflects it, both at once.

What makes this so hard to talk about is that words can't be counted on to say what they seem to be saying. There is overwhelming evidence that many of the ten million Americans who've bought Springsteen's *Born in the U.S.A.* album regard the title song as an expression of unmitigated patriotism, even though the lyrics express a Vietnam vet's tremendous bitterness for what his country has done to him. President Reagan wins praise for his strong stance against terrorism at the same time that he throws all his prestige into fighting for money for the Contras in Nicaragua, who of course are terrorists, even to the extent of intentionally killing innocent civilians. This makes no sense but Reagan gets away with it, and friends of mine, who seem in other respects to be ethical, caring human beings, say they support him wholeheartedly. I notice I don't even like to think about this subject, because the frustration and powerlessness I feel are so great. Jackson Browne has a new song that attempts to address this issue head-on:

"As if freedom was a question of might/As if loyalty was black and white/You hear people say it all the time —/'My country wrong or right' / I want to know what that's got to do / With what it takes to find out what's true / With everyone from the President on down / Trying to keep it from you."

The song, *For America,* is a hit and is being played a lot on all rock radio formats and on music television. It's a powerful song, well-crafted to achieve a specific purpose: reopen the debate, get people to think, feel, react. And yet in the present environment one can't help wondering how many people just hear the chorus — "I have prayed for America/I was made for America/It's in my blood and in my bones" — and a few phrases out of context ("rockets' red glare," "land of the free"), and believe they're hearing more right-on patriotism, good old Jackson, he loves this country too, go Reagan, yay team. It's well-known that President Reagan embraced the song *Born in the U.S.A.* and its singer as examples of the new spirit in this country when he ran for reelection in 1984. Senator Bill Bradley of New Jersey bills himself as the world's biggest Springsteen fan, and he voted for aid to the Contras. Jackson Browne is not unaware of this problem — he speaks of "a generation's blank stare" — and it's to his credit that he's willing to join the fray and do his best to use the media for what he believes in. The risk on the one hand is failure to communicate, the humiliation of being ignored or

misinterpreted, and on the other hand the risk is he'll
succeed in communicating and will be perceived as a
politician rather than a creative artist or an entertainer,
as happened to Jane Fonda for a while. Certainly many
will accuse him of being heavy-handed. I think he's a
shining example, myself—someone who cares enough
about America and rock and roll to try to get both of
them to live up to their ideals.

My favorite recent topical rock song (though not one
that's likely to be as helpful in winning hearts and
minds as Jackson's effort to convert love for country
into a force for the good) is Bruce Cockburn's *If I Had
A Rocket Launcher*. This one also alludes to Nicaragua
and U.S. intervention and issues of human rights and
life and death, and it does a great job of fulfilling one of
rock's classic purposes: the release of anger. Some have
complained that the song promotes violence; I feel
rather that it tells the truth about the singer's feelings:
"Here comes the helicopter / Second time today /
Everybody scatters / And hopes it goes away / How
many kids they've murdered / Only God can say / If I
had a rocket launcher / I'd make somebody pay." Cockburn is a skillful songwriter, and he uses words and
melody very well; this song manages a powerful, controlled rock and roll sound which fits perfectly with
lyrics and tune, building and building until by the end
of the song I'm screaming the appropriately shocking
last words: "If I had a rocket launcher/Some son of a
bitch would die!" People really do feel these feelings —
even pacifists — and it works a lot better to scream
them out while listening to a rock and roll song than to
bury them and pretend they're not there and thus lose
touch with other people's humanity as well as your own.

I bought the Violent Femmes album *(The Blind Leading the Naked*, good title) and immediately fell in love with them thanks to the first three songs on the record, especially the second, *No Killing,* without which either of the other two might seem to lean too far in their respective odd directions.

The first song is a 29-second rave-up called *Old Mother Reagan* ("she's so dumb/she's so dangerous/how come she don't go far away?"), startling, aggressive, and astonishingly commmunicative (again, of a feeling, rather than a position or an idea) for its brief length. Its abrupt ending communicates the singer's conviction that there is right and wrong and we're responsible for our actions — "Old mother Reagan/went to heaven/but at the pearly gates she was stopped" — and sets up an extraordinary transition (one suspects that these two particular sounds have never before been placed one after the other in a musical performance, and it works, not just the first time but over and over and over again, a great example of what Richard Meltzer once called an "unknown tongue") into *No Killing*: "We don't want no killing, Lord; I don't want to see my brother die."

I love this song. I think they could have ended it about thirty seconds earlier — apart from that, it's perfect. First of all, it has something to say, something wrenched up from deep in the gut, a scream from deep inside the collective human unconscious. It resonates. It makes a strong moral statement, and, as a successful work of rock music must, it makes that statement not only in words but by creating a totally compelling sound: the power of the vocals, the simplicity and intricacy of the structural changes, the harmonies between voices, between instruments, between voices and instruments, the beat (the several different beats that come and go in the course of the song), the surprising shifts in mood, attitude, direction of the narrative (a narrative in which the sound of the singer's voice plays as big a part as the words he sings) — from "we don't want no killing" to "loneliness is all around" to "I think it's the Milwaukee police!" to "no killing" again with a group instead of individual emphasis to "every day I need your love." It's one of those beautiful works of music that can be listened to again and again without losing its quality of mystery — or its power to call forth strong emotions — presumably because it is not a mental construct but something closer to a spontaneous inspiration (or a series of inspirations whipped together into a song at another inspired moment). This is creation on the edge, over the edge. I can't explain or justify the running together of this strong and simple moral statement with the personal, almost hysterical paranoia of the "polizei" section, with the combined joy and desperation of the "I need your love" section... all I know is I like having them together. It has an almost otherworldy rightness to it, and also one of its appeals is that it is so individualistic, it expresses Gordon Gano and the Violent Femmes, no one else would have done it like this, and somehow that also means it expresses and was made for me. This gets into what I call the "fait accompli" in rock songs — because the Beatles laugh at the end of *Within You Without You,* you and I as listeners must and will, consciously or unconsciously, create a context, a feeling, an appropriateness or integration for that song and that laughter — you can say, "they shouldn't have laughed," but the laughter is there on the record, and approve or disapprove you as listener will now integrate it into your experience of side two of *Sgt. Pepper* and make it work, probably make it work in some way that neither the Beatles nor you could ever have conceived of consciously. The part of each of us that experiences music has ways of "understanding" that are quite beyond the reach or comprehension of our conscious minds.

Third song: *Faith.* Rumor has it the Femmes are born-again Christians. This song in any case is quite explicit about the singer's beliefs: "I believe in the Father/I believe in the Son/I believe there's a Spirit for everyone." And, "Got my faith, baby, in the Lord/And I know/He'll make everything alright." It's a joyful, loose, Dixieland number (sax, trombone, piano, organ, harmonica), complete with call and response, goofy at times, fiercely smart at times, and so unaffected and sincere throughout that it's hard to imagine anyone disapproving. (Six years ago, when Bob Dylan embraced "born-again" Christianity, the response of the rock audience was so hostile that he found himself unable to sell out 3000-seat theatres, when a year before he'd been playing very successfully in 15,000-seaters. But that was six years ago, and Dylan, true to his nature, was angry and righteous about his new beliefs, "I've found it and you haven't." The Femmes, although anger is also one of their specialties, don't seem to be angry at their audience — and anyway Christian conversion is too common in rock and roll these days to be totally unfashionable, even in punk/-new wave/avant garde rock circles. If the Femmes do lose their old audience it will only be because they're becoming popular — album in the top 100, rave review in *People* magazine – acceptance by the mass audience is the one unforgivable sin out on the rock fringe.)

I like the swinging sound of the song, I like the originality and unpredictableness of its structure, I like the message, I like the vocal, and I like above all the conviction of this band, it really means something to me when a band sounds like what they have to say to me means more to them than how many records they sell or how good their chops are or when the next ounce of coke is going to arrive.

I like a band that cares about something, and that naturally brings me to one of my other favorite songs of the moment, the title track from Faith No More's first album *We Care A Lot*. This is really a wonderful recording, possibly as dumb as *Wild Thing* and a lot funnier. The lead vocal and chorus are perfect – great deadpan attitude, they sound like the ultimate generic all-inclusive rock band, like Spinal Tap (if you haven't seen the movie *Spinal Tap* go down to the video store right now and rent a copy; every rock band I've met in recent years totally identifies with this group and this movie; ostensibly it's a send-up of heavy metal, but there's a certain level where it all comes together and every band's experience is the same, and funny/dumb is also sad, sweet, and true). The arrangement, the clomp-clomp rhythm section and bursts of fuzz guitar, works great – again, not just because it's funny but also because it's inspired, they've achieved exactly the sound that God intended this record to have three billion years ago when He created the universe. It slides into my brain just right and goes clunk!, every time – that's what I mean by a good sound, in case you were wondering.

"We care a lot about disasters, fires, floods and killer bees/We care a lot about Los Angeles falling in the sea/We care a lot about starvation and the food that Live Aid bought/We care a lot about disease, baby, Rock, Hudson, Rock!"

How can I love a song that mocks everything I admire in contemporary rock and roll? How can I not love it, you mean. Faith No More have got our number, but good. "We care a lot about you people, yeah, you bet we care a lot." And the chorus: "It's a dirty job but someone's gotta do it..."

The new Stones album, *Dirty Work*, lacks the commitment of Jackson Browne, the irreverence of Faith No More, the passion of Bruce Cockburn, and the sheer energy and inventiveness of the Violent Femmes, but it does have a certain charm of its own. There's even a song with some moral content, of sorts — a tune called *Winning Ugly*, in which Jagger, if he indeed wrote the lyrics, acknowledges that his morals and values are essentially on a par with those of record company execs and government officials — "I wanna be on top/forever on the up/and damn the competition/I never play it fair/I never turn a hair/just like the politicians/I wanna win that cup and get my money, baby.../ And we're winning, winning ugly" — and wonders, "How can I live my life this way?" The song is not ironic or sarcastic, thankfully (on the other hand the inner sleeve comic about the bitch aerobics instructor and the fat people I take to be an expression of contempt for the Stones' audience, and no, I don't appreciate it), which just goes to show that these issues and concerns are surfacing everywhere.

The song I like best on this record so far is *One Hit (to the Body),* which uses the now very-clichéd analogy between love and drug addiction, with a lot of boxing imagery added in...but clichés are not necessarily a bad thing in rock, and somehow this song (perhaps because the Stones, Keith in particular, have real experience in this area) carries considerable conviction. I mean, it may sound like I'm being very analytical, but actually all it is is I hear conviction in one song and not in another—I feel the power, and then maybe I make some guesses about how come it's there. Your guess is as good as mine, of course. Anyway, it's tempting to put aside the analogy, and take the song as literally being about Keith's love affair with heroin (or even booze). Heard this way, it's quite affecting. "The smell of your flesh excites me/my blood starts to flow/so help me God." Again, no irony, no pose. Just reporting. This is how it is. "One round took me out of the game / you did me some permanent harm." "I don't need no security / I just need me some peace."

Now of course this imagery does apply to and can be very evocative in relation to a love affair. It depends to an extent on the needs of the listener. For myself, the song seems more powerful when I strip away its multiple meanings and let it just be about what it's pretending to be about. I find myself going back to Lou Reed's classic Velvet Underground track, *Heroin,* which because it is so straightforwardly about heroin allows itself be about so much more. This song predates and is simpler than *Sister Ray*: "I don't know just where I'm going/but I'm gonna try for the kingdom if I can..." It's an extraordinarily romantic song, which may seem objectionable in a song about heroin use, but as in *Rocket*

Launcher, sometimes you have to put your ideas about things aside and just hear and acknowledge the truth about how people sometimes feel. "I wish that I was born a thousand years ago/I wish that I'd sailed the darkened seas on a great big clipper ship..." "Oh and I guess that I just don't know." "Heroin/will be the death of me." What the singer of the song is reaching for is bigger than heroin, but heroin is what he's found, and what he wants to communicate is that, dead end that it is, it's still so much bigger and more rewarding than the rest of what he sees around him. He also subtly acknowledges something you can hear clearly in the Violent Femmes' songs, and that might even be there in *One Hit (to the Body),* which is that I know you're afraid of me, and I wish it wasn't so, 'cause I'm lonely, but fuck you anyway, asshole. "Thank your God that I'm not aware/and thank God that I just don't care."

Maybe beneath the cool, tough, wasted Keith-Richards-image at the center of the *Dirty Work* cover there's a Keith who'd like to be loved for something other than being cool, tough and wasted (and doesn't dare – "I know that the world is starved for love," say the Femmes). Maybe not. Certainly Ronald Reagan and company, or if not them then those masters of war Dylan sings about (and yes, I do believe they exist), thank their God that we're not aware and thank God that we just don't care. They may even think God wants their money and buys their act, same as everyone else.

This isn't about who's right and who's wrong. This is actually about greater compassion. And a change of attitude. It's coming. You can hear it in the music.

Chapter Ten

"And when our hearts return to ashes/It'll be just a story."
— Yoko Ono

Now I feel, as much as I have ever been, in the middle of rock and roll. Prince's brand new album is on my stereo, last night I saw the Jesus and Mary Chain in San Francisco, I just taped an interview with my friend Michael about what it's like to be a rock reporter for *Rolling Stone* (he talked about his experience backstage at Live Aid, and I remembered myself at Woodstock), and next week I have hopes of spending four or five days on tour with the Violent Femmes. But take away all this activity, and I'd still be in the same place: surrounded by new music and feelings stimulated by the music. The heart of the beast. This is where I was heading when I started on this journey, not sure whether I could make it at age 37 or whether there was really a "here" to get to in 1980s rock.

Well, there is. I'm measuring it by the same yardstick I used back in the 1960s, when I truly was too much of an idiot to even pretend I knew anything, and the only way I could measure the Stones or Jefferson Airplane or Hendrix or the scene as a whole was by my own experience and feelings. Something would excite me, and I'd want to tell my friends. There was nothing professional about pressing my ear up against a speaker to glory in the bass line on *Viola Lee Blues* (first Grateful Dead album, they weren't afraid to make records in those days) or turning the volume past the pain point on the headphones to scream out my jealous rage at an ex-girlfriend with the help of *I Can See for Miles* (the Who). I was an amateur and loving it, even as the press came around to interview the teenage rock and roll expert. It occurs to me that that's what I saw last night watching the Jesus and Mary Chain: brilliant inspired amateurs, kids who've discovered a new sound, and a new variation on an old attitude, and they're out there dancing in the midst of the chaos, answering to their own muse and playing by private rules, breaking new ground because they're too young and full of themselves to learn what anyone with more experience could tell them, that this isn't the way to make music. The Velvet Underground were such amateurs, and so were the Beatles, and when the dust settled after the stampede was done (one group seemingly brought down by commercial success, the other by commercial failure, but the truth of the matter lies elsewhere, as simple and complex as what happened to the Beach Boys or the Sex Pistols), Lou Reed and Paul McCartney were set up for long careers as accomplished old pros who could never quite escape the shadow of what they achieved when they were still too dumb to know better.

I have a strong bias against "professionalism" in rock and roll. Neil Young's phrase "out of the blue and into the black" is a good description of how the process works for most rock acts: one day you're nobody, the next day you're the latest money machine and there's all sorts of weird creatures around you trying to hitch a ride on your meteorite. This is true even if, like Creedence, you were toiling in the rock and roll fields for ten years before your "overnight" success. And usually when you hit, it's either by accident (and you disappear again fast) or it's because you've stumbled onto (or carefully, consciously created) a new sound which the world, without knowing it, has been waiting for, starving for. That thing which you arrive with, the song and the sound that puts you on the map, whether it's *Please Please Me* or *Little Red Corvette* or *Proud Mary* or *Surfin' Safari* or *Light My Fire* or *Shop Around* or *Heartbreak Hotel* or *Blowin' in the Wind* or *I Will Follow,* is almost by definition the creation of an amateur. No one knows how to make successful or popular music until they're already doing it, and even then you're just a gambler on a roll: some people stay hot for an incredibly long time, but they're the exception. Most rock musicians have been very popular or very good or both only for brief periods. It's like getting a tiger by the tail, and holding on or swinging it around you as long as you can, and the moment you pause to take a breath, goodbye.

"Professionalism" to me (and I admit this is an attitude, and a contradictory and inconsistent one at that) implies that a person thinks they know how to do what they do, and that there are certain objective standards that can and should be applied: you stay in tune, you keep the beat, you hit the high notes, you talk nice to the radio station people, you milk the encores. To me, whenever you think you know what you're doing and how to do it, you have in effect reached the limits of your creativity. You may well please a lot of the people a lot of the time, and that certainly counts for something; but my prejudice is that what I want in rock and roll is that it go for broke, keep taking chances, fall on its face again and again and sometimes ring the bell of genius.

And what I like about it is that somehow it's set up, this form of music, this conceptual or cultural setting where the music is made, whatever it is, it's set up so that this does go on happening. The Violent Femmes and Elvis Costellos and U2s and Princes and LL Cool Js and Tears for Fears and Translators and Los Loboses and R.E.M.s do keep bursting on the scene, new voices new ideas new energy new music, some make money and some don't, some go on being brilliant and some get corrupted or just run out of steam, but the process is alive, I find it to be as fertile and productive and rewarding and stimulating in 1986 as it was in 1967 or any other year I have any experience of. And I said before, and will try to explain myself a little further now, that I believe that for all its pitfalls top 40 radio, and the very commerciality and competitiveness and transitory nature of rock and roll that the top 40 concept promotes, may be the single most important factor in rock's continuing health and its survival as a creative environment.

It's hard to believe that top 40, or what is currently called CHR (Contemporary Hit Radio), can possibly be a vital creative stimulus when you look at the records that are actually on the charts at any particular moment. They tend to run the gamut from awful to mediocre, and if there's one song that's really worth listening to or one hit video worth watching at any given moment you can probably consider yourself lucky. Furthermore, as I write this the news media are just starting to break the story of the incredible network of corruption and payola and protection money that keeps records on (and off) the playlists of CHR stations in the U.S., with plenty of mob involvement and enough scandal to keep the investigators and congressional hearings busy for years, if they dare (the music business is basically small potatoes, and easy to pick on, but organized crime is something else). And isn't the easy money generated by hit records (and the desire for it) the most destructive force in the world of rock and roll, along with the drugs that easy money buys?

Yes, certainly; I can't argue with the proposition that top 40 radio (along with its equivalent formats: top 40 music TV, top 40 black radio, top 40 "album-oriented-rock" radio, top 40 soft rock and so forth) is a destructive force. But it shouldn't seem so strange to us to find the destructive and the creative lying in the same bed. Shiva the Destroyer is also the Life-Giver. The relentlessly commercial orientation of rock and roll spawns a multitude of horrors, but it does promote an ambition to communicate along with an ambition to be well-paid. When people buy your records or come to your shows, you know you've reached them in some fashion.

Noncommercial art forms (opera, modern classical music, dance, literary writing) tend to be dominated by an elite of critics and academics. Critics have a role in rock music, and I acknowledge that most of the really

satisfying music I've found in my current exploration of
the rock scene has been music the critics like, their lists
and reviews have helped guide me to the good stuff.
But the great thing about rock critics is that they're not
very powerful—and they're poorly paid. Since their
power, if any, is mainly to help call attention to new
bands, they're a lot less corrupt and less hidebound
than they would be if they actually determined what
records get made and who gets to perform. And because they're poorly paid, there's a healthy turnover in
their ranks, and most of the time most of the critics are
doing what they do primarily for love of music.

Rock escapes the stagnation that we see in the twentieth century in most if not all noncommercial art forms
by existing in the rough and tumble world of the
marketplace. This world is full of inequities and cor-
rupting forces, but it also in many cases rewards innovation (Prince, the Beatles, the Beach Boys, Talking
Heads), sincerity (Springsteen, U2), and talent (Dylan,
Stevie Wonder, Aretha Franklin). Above all, it is a
world that is regularly invaded by the unexpected. The
vehicle for that invasion, in the most striking cases
(Elvis, the Beatles, recently the Police, Prince, and
Springsteen), is hit-oriented radio (and TV). The opportunity is there to come from outside and seize the
airwaves and rewrite the rules, and it is done again and
again—more in the Eighties and Sixties than in the
Seventies, which is why the Seventies is viewed as a
relatively stagnant time for rock music.

When I try to imagine rock and roll without its
charts, without the weekly countdowns that so fascinate
my eleven-year-old and thirteen-year-old (I was the
same way at their age), without the fierce ambition to

"hit the top" that corrupts in most cases but inspires in the best cases...when I try to imagine rock and roll going along from year to year without the popularity circus, the haircuts, the fan magazines, and the rebel lions against those things, the fashionable anti-fashions like punk and heavy metal, when I try to imagine a rock and roll measuring itself somehow solely on artistic or musical merit...I see a music of diminishing returns, possibly flowering briefly in a flourish of creative freedom, but quickly becoming lost and divided against itself. The ambitious need something to aspire to, and a door which, even if locked, can be broken through at times. The underground needs an overground to separate itself from and thus define itself by.

It's a crazy system, but it works. And it brings people in. I wouldn't be listening to Translator or the Violent Femmes today if I hadn't heard Tears for Fears on hit radio last summer.

And bands like Translator or Green on Red, while they often fear and reject commercial success if it means being packaged like Starship or Heart, would love to be successful on their own terms, and may even look to bands like the Beatles – than whom no one was more commercial, as it turned out – as models in that respect. There is, in other words, a kind of rock and roll dream, in which you can make it by being yourself, and make a difference in the world by doing so. Most bands won't realize this dream in a big way, but that doesn't change the dream's power as a motivator.

Take away the top 40, however – take away rock and roll's doorway to true mass communication – and you take away the dream, the possibility of hitting the jackpot and working large-scale miracles. And you might

180/   *The Map*
180/ The Map

find that all you have left is people's sketchy ideas of what rock and roll is, musically, formally. You wouldn't have the rock and roll environment any more.

There is no kind of professionalism that can sustain rock and roll in the intensity and creativity and rebelliousness that give it whatever meaning it has for us. As long as rock and roll continues to be a place where brilliant amateurs can break in and kick over the statues and make their mark and blaze new trails, it will stand. I'm not saying top 40 radio is the only way this can happen — already that's not true, and in fact there have always been other routes. I'm just saying that top 40 and the opportunities it offers despite the crap it usually delivers, has been and continues to be a vital unifying force. Not everything on the Hot 100 chart (Hot 100 = top 40, it's a concept, not a number) is rock and roll, by a longshot. But rock has been at home on, and indeed has dominated, the pop charts for three decades, and in its own weird way this home has served rock well.

The other thing I need to say is that the short, intense life-span of a hit single — in your ears all the time for two or three months, and then gone to oldie heaven — is the basis of rock's identification with "what's happening," this is where we get the idea that a new song is or can be a message from and to the collective human consciousness. This is a vital part of rock's self-image. And it is a wonderful medium in which to create. "Come on," say Tears for Fears, "I'm talking to you. Shout! Shout! Let it all out. These are the things we can do without..." It's a vague, safe, unfocused political message — but it has the possibility of being very specific, even dangerous, at a time when many people are feeling the same frustrations and are ready to act on or express them. Equally vague songs in the 1960s ("Stop, hey, what's that sound/everybody look what's going down") seemed extremely pointed, for some of us, in the context in which they were heard. "We don't want no killing, Lord..." Music has always been universal; but rock is a music born in and created for the global media. It cuts across boundaries, it associates itself not with space but with time. It speaks in and for the moment. Now. Now. Now.

¤

At the heart of the rock beast lies something very personal for each one of the hundreds of millions of us who listen to this stuff. There was a time in my life when no one except the music seemed to understand me. I don't suppose the music could ever mean quite that much to me again, unless I were again that hungry, that confused, that lonely. It's interesting that I wouldn't wish that on myself or anyone, and yet out of that circumstance comes an intensity of experience that we then yearn for for the rest of our lives.

Personal means private. You and I may agree on the power of a particular song, but what each of us hears in the song is necessarily different. Necessarily, because the source of the song's real power lies in a kind of bond it makes with each person's private and unique experience and perception. If a rock and roll song or any work of creative art fails to bond with the individual listener in this fashion, it lacks real power for that person. (It may have instead a kind of power by association or reputation, but that is always an "emperor's new clothes" situation. What we respond to in such a case is not the emperor's clothes but the response we perceive others making to those clothes. Their response moves us, not the music or art itself.)

I use the word "personalize" to refer to the process of bonding that takes place between the listener and the song (or performance or recording or painting or whatever it is). This is not a conscious process, nor is it a passive one. It may occur the first time you hear a song, or it may build up over the course of repeated listenings; or it may occur on one particular occasion when you hear the song, even though you've heard it a number of times before. In other words, it can be either a gradual process or a sudden one, or both together.

When I personalize a song, it means that in some sense I hear it as being about me. It may not be the lyrics I hear this way—very often it's the sound of the song, as it was when I heard *Ticket to Ride* on the radio in the senior room my last year in high school. Now you (or I) can speculate about what "sound" it was that caught my attention, connected for me—it might have been the guitar, or the particular inflection of the vocal, or that interesting, shuffling beat, or the combination of all three. But since I'm the one who heard it, there's no way you can know for sure, no matter how much of a Beatles expert, or rock expert, or adolescent expert you are. And the thing is, I don't know for sure either. Was it her eyes, or the dress she wore that day? All I really remember is that I fell in love.

¤

This evening I went out to the garage, where I keep all the records I never listen to any more but would never consider getting rid of, and grabbed a copy of *Crosby, Stills and Nash*. I put it on the phonograph. It was like hearing it for the first time. What an extraordinary album! What a sound they created, nothing quite like it before or since, truly timeless (like the first Doors album) and utterly of the moment. I didn't expect to be so moved.

Everybody knows this record. Yesterday I dropped by Translator's practice room in Berkeley, and we drove over to look at a motor home their manager is considering fixing up for them for their upcoming national tour. (The guys were excited about it.) Afterwards, standing on the sidewalk, Bob was examining the cherry-like fruit on a nearby tree and Larry said, "Can I have some of your purple berries?" Bob replied, without missing a beat, "Yeah, I've been eating them for six or seven weeks now." That song (*Wooden Ships*) and the other nine from the album are engraved on the insides of more minds than I care to think about.

Acoustic guitars and gorgeous soprano harmonies. What makes this rock and roll? Context, for want of a better answer. Rock music is much more a context in which new music is created, than it is a set of rules. Crosby, Stills and Nash were veterans of three excellent and innovative Sixties rock groups, the Byrds, Buffalo Springfield, and the Hollies, and they started hanging out with each other and singing together, just sitting around the living room. And it's like you're sitting there, putting your voice together with these two other voices, and suddenly you're hearing this sound you've never heard before in your life, like God is in the room, some kind of very powerful magic. What are you going to do? Well, you could run as fast as possible in the other direction, but these guys were adventurous musicians and the timing was right, in terms of their careers and the energy of the moment and all that stuff,

184/   *The Map*

and so they made a record together—inspired by the harmony of their voices and their personalities, their personal and musical camaraderie, to do the best work of their careers, their lives. There was this feeling in the air of being on the edge of a new millennium, the end of an old world and the beginning of a new one, so real you could touch it. I was there. I attended some of the sessions, David and I wrote some songs together that didn't get on the album. I remember a small party in David's house, I think this was before they started recording, the three of them sang Paul McCartney's *Blackbird*, Steven picking it out on an acoustic guitar. Gooseflesh. It was chilling, unforgettable.

I was reading in the latest *Rolling Stone* an account by John Phillips (of the Mamas and Papas) of his $1000-a-day cocaine/heroin/barbiturate addiction and the circumstances of his arrest in 1980 as a drug dealer. It made me think of the long articles about David Crosby that I read in *Spin* and *Rolling Stone* last year, of how years and years of freebasing cocaine had turned David into a kind of living zombie whom none of his friends could reach or help, a man who'd been busted repeatedly and faced hard time in a Texas prison and whose death was constantly predicted by even his closest friends, who still somehow had the strength to defy the world, friend and foe alike, and go on with his habit, bitterly denouncing everyone who'd lost faith in him along the way.

David was a friend of mine—still is, although I haven't seen him for a long time (he's in prison as I write this—was on the lam again for a while but ultimately turned himself in). He was always a stubborn bastard—proud and insecure, courageous and fiercely idealistic. I disliked him the first time I met him, but he came to be one of the few musicians of that era that I really enjoyed spending time with, he had a brilliant mind and could listen as well as talk, and underneath or alongside all his vanity he could be incredibly vulnerable, really open himself and share his heart with his friends, with the people around him. He had a beautiful heart, David Crosby — maybe he still does.

The thing that strikes me about his addiction is how strong he's been, in a perverse way. Maybe he'll be dead by the time you read this, maybe he'll still be alive, maybe prison will even straighten him out (though it failed the first few times), but the point is that anyone else would have been dead years ago. I think of cocaine as a parasite. In David it found an extraordinary host — a man with little will to resist the drug itself, and an indomitable will to survive and, ultimately, to resist everyone and everything that tried to separate him from his habit.

Why am I talking about this? Drugs and alcohol play a huge part in the history of rock and roll, as they do in the history of jazz. Today there are major figures in the rock world who are known for not being drug users or drinkers: Prince and his band, Springsteen, U2, Mellencamp now, and others. This is news, this comes almost as a surprise, and it suggests that the music may survive, that it may be possible to be a risk-taking, highly creative rock and roller exposed to the roller coaster of performing and fame and the business and all the pressures — and yet not succumb to the temptations that have killed or severely damaged so many rock stars in the past, and that are still killing 'em or rendering 'em useless today.

The music has survived this long, however, and that brings up an unpleasant thought: maybe the addictive drugs, including of course alcohol, that have killed or crippled so many rock musicians, have actually in some way helped make rock and roll what it is. Even today, of course, many of the best of the up-and-coming bands are famous for their alcoholic excesses, including the Replacements, Los Lobos, the Jesus & Mary Chain. Bands play in clubs, my friend Larry points out, and clubs make their money serving alcohol. Bands that bring in a drinking crowd are a lot more likely to get work than bands that don't. And the creative ethic that I espouse, risk-taking, spontaneity, go for broke, is one that many creative people need (or believe they need) alcohol or drugs to achieve. Spontaneous, uninhibited, unpredictable creativity is often referred to as Dionysian, after the God of wine and revelry.

The *Spin* article on Crosby reads like very impressive journalism, but I was surprised to find numerous factual errors in it regarding people and events of the 1960s. Musicians are placed in the wrong bands, and so forth. Talking of Crosby, Stills, Nash & Young at Woodstock (summer '69), the article says, "In those halcyon days, David only smoked marijuana and dreamed of owning a sailboat." In fact, David had had his sailboat for several years at that point, and he was already seriously into cocaine at the CSN recording sessions earlier that year. That was my first taste of the stuff, and I remember doing coke and then writing song after song — many of 'em quite good, or anyway better and less inhibited than anything I'd done before. Fortunately for me, I'm not a very addictive type, and also I never had the money to dabble very seriously in coke. (As a result, I stayed straight enough to notice early on how incredibly destructive it could be if used repeatedly — I got into arguments in those days with people who claimed it wasn't addictive, I could see plenty of first-hand evidence to the contrary.)

Money. If you think of cocaine as an entity, a demon or maybe a parasitic invader from some other reality, you have to admire what it achieved in Crosby's case. It definitely helped him to make the album that directly (royalties) and indirectly (reputation) provided him with the money to feed his very expensive coke habit nonstop for the next sixteen years. I think it's a mimicking kind of parasite — in the interviews with Crosby, it still sounds like the David I knew, same mannerisms, same attitudes, only you can tell it's really the drug talking. It says the only thing it cares about is music, man — but it says it in a way that seems only designed to help it, the drug that lives inside and controls the man, go on surviving. Tell 'em what they want to hear. Strike a good pose. Keep up the facade. Tell 'em you quit completely. Slip into the next room for another hit.

The drug took his strength and his pride and used them to seal him off from anyone who could help him. It's a fascinating and horrible process. The invasion of the body-snatchers.

And here's this beautiful, beautiful record that will live forever, and that helped to destroy at least one of the people who created it. It really is hard to know what to think about this. Should I in fact tell people how fabulous Los Lobos are in live performance? Maybe I'm just speeding up the process of their self-destruction by doing so.

One thing I want to avoid, in any case, is promoting the myth of the musician as victim. It's true that there are a lot of blood-sucking, money-grabbing business persons floating around the rock world, and that the bad blood often drives out the good, having more patience since it has no heart. (I actually gave up on being with David Crosby very early, not because of drugs directly but because I was too proud myself to spend hours or days hanging around waiting for him to give me his attention. He'd invite me to work on something with him, and then... Michael Goldberg recently wrote a profile of Stevie Wonder in which he reveals that Stevie's life is full of people waiting around for him, people he invited to him with good and sincere intentions except he's always running six hours or six months behind schedule... It's easy to see why rock stars, or movie stars, or politicians, end up with no one around them except those who stand to make money from being there or who have nothing better to do.) But it does no good to sing songs of self-reliance and then portray yourself (or let yourself be portrayed) as the victim of your managers, your record company, your fans, whatever. Somehow one has to find a way around all that, keep finding ways, or else self-reliance becomes nothing more than a pose, a lie. Preaching the power of the individual and living a life of irresponsibility, indulgence, and powerlessness, ain't gonna further the revolution.

I saw John Cougar Mellencamp last night at the Oakland Coliseum, and I had a great time, and I really like and respect the guy now. He's his own man, and he cares about his audience, and it really is so easy to see when those things are true and not just a fashionable pose or something the performer dearly wants to believe about himself. People who are self-reliant and who do know that what they're here for is to give and receive love, always find ways to cut through the bullshit that ties everyone else in knots. One example: Mellencamp put on the first arena show I've been to that provided kick-ass rock and roll without being so loud that you could only feel, not hear, the music. He got a marvelous sound, the sound of a really tight local band, garage band, bar band, that loves rock and roll and knows how to get people dancing.

And when he did his little pitch about the American farmer, and writing to your Congressman – I'd heard about this, and what he said was real simplistic and all that, but the thing is he was talking right to me, and meant what he was saying. And when he said that what's going on with the farmers is like this, the super-big farm corporations have engineered things in such a way as to destroy and get rid of the little guys – I got it, I realized he's right, that's exactly what's happening, it is that simple, and what you can do about it if anything is not raise money but spread the truth, get the word out. And he's doing it. A hundred shows, ten or fifteen thousand people at each show, and he talks to them from the heart in a context where they're open and listening and it's person to person (not like TV – he's really there)...it makes a difference. And the guy rocks, and he loves music, and I gotta say I just really appreciate him.

I still might not buy his album, but that's not the important thing. The important thing is that he is who he says he is. And that might be the most dangerous thing about alcohol and drugs, and professionalism: they can keep you from being who you say you are.

Chapter Eleven

"Got to try a new position..."

— Prince

Translator left today on the first leg of a two-month tour of clubs and colleges. They go up the coast to Portland, Vancouver, and Seattle, then return to the Bay Area to kick off an itinerary that is fairly staggering: Santa Cruz; Cotati; Salt Lake City; Columbia; Lincoln; Iowa City; Minneapolis; Madison; Milwaukee; Chicago; Detroit; Lansing; Cincinatti; Pittsburgh; Washington, DC; Asbury Park; Hoboken; Providence; Northhampton; Burlington; Boston; New Haven; New York City. That's 23 gigs in 30 days, sometimes playing several shows a night, and they'll do almost as many more as they make the southern swing back across the United States — the bookings are still being made, but they'll probably hit Louisville, Atlanta, Houston, Austin, Tucson, Los Angeles, and plenty of places in between. They'll travel with three friends, Dal, Floyd, and Zombie — road manager, sound man, and guitar roadie, respectively—in two vehicles. When they're not performing, sleeping, hanging out backstage, or driving, they'll be doing interviews at college radio stations or catching a meal at a strange restaurant in a strange town. It's an open question right now whether they'll earn any money beyond expenses for two months' hard labor away from home in claustrophobic conditions, but maybe they'll call some attention to their new record, and if the record sells they'll get paid a little better for the next tour, which could start (if the record sells) a few days after this one ends. The important thing, anyway, is that for a few hours each day they'll be doing the one thing that each of these guys lives for: playing their music, Translator music, in front of an audience. Sometimes it seems like touring is a means to an end — money, success—but for these guys, and for a lot of the musicians I've met, it's more the other way around: the purpose of success is to make it possible for you to go on playing your music on the road. All of the effort — the songwriting, the practicing, the interviews, the business dealings and everything else—culminates and becomes meaningful at the moment of performance, sometimes in a recording studio but mostly on some stage somewhere, in a (hopefully) crowded bar or college gym or concert hall, whatever they offer you, whatever space is appropriate for the number of people that you can draw at this instant in your (probably) brief career. It's all for that moment of performance, which comes and goes like that, and leaves behind at best something intangible, something like self-knowledge or joy or a memory of intensity, in the hearts of (some of) the people who saw the show. You the performer will never know for sure who you touched or how or how deeply. But you know how you felt when you were on stage, and you know that for now anyway you're living and working to be in that moment again.

A couple of nights ago I danced on stage at a Violent Femmes gig. Usually I like to be out in the audience, watching the musicians' faces and feeling the music and the energy of the crowd wash over me, but I was tired and the club (One Step Beyond, in Santa Clara) was very crowded and I'd been in the audience at the last two Femmes shows (University of California at Davis, a big hall, no seats, and the Warfield in San Francisco, a handsome old theater, all reserved seating). All of the people in the band and on the tour had been very friendly to me, after four days I felt like part of the tour, so I felt little inhibition about standing there towards the back, stage left, in full view of the audience — I figured if the bouncers standing on stage weren't a distraction, then I wouldn't be either.

At first I just wanted to see what the gig and the audience looked like from the musicians' point of view. And then of course the music caught me up, as it had the other two nights, and I was doing what Caleb, the sound guy, called, "the Femmes shuffle." (I guess I *was* somewhat inhibited, or simply tired, because at the Warfield I'd been jumping up and down in front of my seat, screaming. At One Step Beyond I was just swaying back and forth, singing along, and shaking my arms at the performers and the audience at appropriate moments.)

And unexpectedly, I didn't just *see* what it looked like from the musicians' perspective, but to some small degree I felt it. What a rush! It has nothing to do with ideas or anything that happens in the mind, because when you're on stage there's no time and also no place for thinking. You feel it, like a shimmering wall of energy, a solid, palpable thing out there where the audience is, that might glow or have a color for one person and for someone else it's physical, touchable, or it's experienced by depth perception or some other sense. It's no more describable than a color or a flavor is describable – it's just there, and in time you come to know it, you love it and you have other feelings too, you have a relationship with it, always changing, always powerful.

It isn't a mass of people out there – it's a mass of people who are collectively giving you their attention. It's their attention you sense rather than the people themselves, and it's a particular form of attention that exists only when people are experiencing the unique stimulation of music. And you also are experiencing music – making it, hearing it, feeling it, being a part of it – as you experience the touch of their attention.

All these elements together go into an experience that is much less personal than I thought – I thought it might be the rush of knowing that it's *your* music they're getting off on, but in truth that's a thought and one seldom has time to think it. I could feel the energy even though I wasn't making the music myself, even though very few people were specifically paying attention to me. Just being in their range of sight, and seeing them face to face, was enough. It's like there's a physical presence there that takes on form, you can reach out and touch it. But you don't, because that would be like stopping, and all you want to do is keep moving with (or sometimes against) the energy, the music.

It's something you'll never feel any other place than on the rock and roll stage, not this particular flavor of it, anyway. I'd say that it's addictive, except that unlike most addictions I know of it is deeply, spiritually satisfying. It fulfills. But it may also leave you hungry, empty, wanting more, which is certainly a primary reason so many musicians turn to drugs and alcohol. It can be hard to sustain the hour-to-hour absence of that energy, that fullness, when you're not on stage.

At the Warfield, after six or seven songs, Gordon Gano, the Violent Femmes' lead singer and songwriter, looked at the audience and said, "You know I like you all, but you are the most *proper* group of people I've seen on this whole tour..." He didn't exactly say we were dead, but he got his point across, and people started to stand up and move. I can remember Grace Slick and other Jefferson Airplaners on the road, constantly urging people (with both sarcasm and direct exhortation) to get out of their seats and start dancing. The Airplane had come out of a dance ballroom scene where what you saw and felt from the stage was this vortex of excited movement, a pulse before you reflecting and hugely amplifying the pulse of the music coming from the stage. And something going on wherever you happened to cast your eyes, a thousand scenes all over the hall. After you've developed a form of communication that works with and rides on dance hall energy, it's hard to be satisfied with sit-down shows.

This seems to be a constant in rock and roll, one of the few — if a band likes a quiet, sit-down audience, if they play better when faced with order than they do when confronted with chaos, they may be great musicians but they're probably not playing rock and roll, or shouldn't be. Rock isn't meant for quiet, controlled environments. The music is loud because it belongs to the twentieth century; it starts with a world of confusion and noise, and attempts to rise above it, drown it out, scream through it, discover and highlight and affirm the beauty amidst the confusion. Rock and roll demands participation. "Get up, stand up!", says Bob Marley (he may be dead, but he'll still say it to you every time you put on his record), and he's expressing not only the essence of rock's political philosophy, but also rock's philosophy of life, of love, and of art. "Soft rock," one of the most popular formats in today's radio wasteland, is a contradiction in terms.

That doesn't mean all true rock songs have to sound like a chainsaw attacking a freight train. Some songs don't even have a beat and still manage to be rock and roll. Sometimes it's a matter of context. There's no hard and fast rules. But if you find yourself turning on the radio and all you want to hear is something that's a) familiar-sounding and b) non-threatening, and this happens more than once or twice a month, you should probably hang up your rock and roll shoes or else quit your job. Anything that can be piped into elevators and department stores is not rock and roll, I don't care if it was written by Chuck Berry and recorded by Bruce Springsteen or Eddie Van Halen, it ain't rock, we've gotta draw the line somewhere.

¤

I saw the Doors when they were still playing in a club—Ondine, in New York, just before their first album was released—and it was extraordinary, what I remember is this great dark rhythmic *sound* that pounded through the room and seemed to swallow up my entire consciousness, no bass player, just organ, electric guitar, drums, and vocals. They did *When the Music's Over (Turn Out the Lights)* and it was more sexual than sex itself, largely improvised, full of bluesy poetry and hammering organ/drums/guitar riffs, Ray and John and Robbie communicating with a telepathic clarity that allowed them freedom verging on total abandon, Jim prowling the stage and howling in angry and ecstatic tongues. The band had a "voyage" structure they used on that song and *The End* and *Gloria,* a place to start and a place to finish and in between you go as far as you can in every direction that occurs to you, and come back, an acid trip, uncontrollable passion within this very conscious, elegant structure, Jim in particular knew how to make full use of the drama of the environment, the situation, the moment, so that every bit of accidental creation seemed brilliantly planned.

At Ondine it was sexual, wild mysterious forces wrestling and shouting in the darkness, much more a function of sound textures than anything visual. Ten months later, *Light My Fire* and the album having topped the charts, I was at the Fillmore East seeing the Doors for the fourteenth or fifteenth time, and the drama now was political and social rather than sexual and personal, but it was the same drama, the same extraordinary improvisation within musical brackets. The room was bigger, a concert hall (with chairs), the sound was not as physical or all-encompassing, but the visual dramatic element had evolved to more than compensate. I knew this show but it was like I'd never seen it or anything like it before, on the edge of my seat or standing in the aisle scarcely daring to breathe the entire time, Ray pushing Jim and Jim pushing Ray and all the incredible energy of change that was in the air in late summer early fall 1967 was gathered in and focused in each organ riff, each swing of the microphone, "I used to play a game, called GO INSANE" and now he's threatening Robbie and the whole theater is right on the edge and then out of sheer necessity and desperation the music punches through to a higher level, full of the power and momentum and uncertainty and crazed daring that we all felt, alone and collectively, as we rode the wild tide of the times.

The Violent Femmes are one of the best bands since the Doors when it comes to working with the theatrical possibilities that rock offers. Gordon Gano is a truly mysterious figure, in the best sense – the sense in which human beings are mysteries, to themselves and each other. He reads from scripture at the beginning of the song *Hallowed Ground*: "the prophet is a fool, the spiritual man is mad, for the multitude of thine iniquity and the great hatred." The abrupt transition from this plain-spoken, provocative reading, into the opening chords of *Hallowed Ground,* and then into the song's opening lyrics ("everyone's trying to decide/where to go when there's no place to hide") is the essence of drama, the sort of drama that brings buried, unexpected feelings to the surface, that works so subtly and unpredictably and powerfully that it can have a different impact every time you hear it. And the man has something to say! Who else has captured nuclear fear this well, who else in rock and roll or contemporary letters has said anything on the subject quite as worthwhile as Gano's couplet: "My hope is in what they can't bring down/My soul is in hallowed ground"? Brian Ritchie's attack on the bass notes, the intelligence and punch of

Victor DeLorenzo's drumming, the gorgeous and eerie
oooings of the backup vocals, the fiery lead guitar solo,
the everchanging inflection of Gano's voice, everything
in this ensemble performance contributes brilliantly to
a growing tension that fascinates, penetrates, hyp-
notizes, takes familiar issues and feelings and makes
them totally new.

Rock and roll performers at their best truly are the
poets/prophets/philosophers of our age. Very few of
them live up to this billing, and those usually only for a
brief time, but what those few produce in their short
time is enough to redeem the entire form, to make it at
least as likely that one will find truth in a record store
or a rock club as in a church or museum or library.
When the Stones released *(I Can't Get No) Satisfaction*
(I remember a disc jockey in upstate New York played
it three times in a row and said it was the new national
anthem), they expressed a truth that was so real for so
many of us that we started looking to the Stones as in-
terpreters and spokespersons for our private and collective realities. When you're surrounded by a cacophony
of nonsense on all sides and you suddenly hear a voice
that makes sense, you naturally turn towards that voice.

Rock's philosophical statements are always conveyed
in the total performance (live or recorded), never in
the words alone. This can be confusing, because the
word phrase "I can't get no satisfaction" *is* the place
where the song's truth is located. The song's power
derives from the statement these words make *plus* the
way the singer sings them (the sound of his voice and
all that that communicates), plus the guitar riff that
plays alongside and within and around these words, plus
the rhythm section that pounds behind, and punctuates

before, between, and after, words and riff. Truth is felt as a visceral response to the words — the statement, "I can't get no satisfaction" — in the context of the overall sound. In a sense the words are a foil, an identifying label, for something bigger that can't be put in words but, through the magic of the performer's art, seems to have been expressed in words anyway. I can remember sitting by a jukebox, pounding on a table in time with the drums while I shouted out the guitar riff. That was my way of saying that I agreed with this philosophical observation.

The philosopher Gordon Gano is 22 years old. He was 20 when he wrote *Hallowed Ground,* and 18 or younger when he wrote his classic songs of teen angst, *Blister in the Sun, Kiss Off,* and *Add It Up,* songs that the kids at Violent Femmes shows greet with wild enthusiasm (like they were getting to hear Led Zeppelin perform *Dazed and Confused* or Bob Dylan sing *Like A Rolling Stone*). "Help me, Lord," he sings on the new album, "help me understand, what it means to be a boy, what it means to be a man." If you haven't heard the song (*I Held Her in My Arms*) I daresay you can't begin to imagine the significance of the tempo at which he sings that, or the way (like so many VF songs) the song plays vocals off against percussion to create its basic structure, and uses the other instrumentation (guitar, sax, bass, organ) to establish a mood — in this case a joyous, nervous mood that wraps itself around the vocals and almost takes charge of what the song says, except then the lyrics start insinuating themselves into the listener's brain and wrap themselves around the impression left by the musical mood, shifting it, changing it (he's remembering a dream, isn't he?) (yes, but not only...). "I will not kill one thing that I love" – uh, sure, but how come you even mention it, what's this guy thinking about anyway? And that drumbeat is so bouncy it's sinister, and so different (from any other rock sound or non-rock sound I can think of) it's subversive. What are these guys up to?

It's interesting. The more, and the more carefully, I listen to the Femmes' songs, the more I hear in them. What's particularly pleasing, along with the depth and quality and effectiveness of what they're doing, is how one-of-a-kind they are. The first time I saw Jim Morrison, all I could think of was how much he looked and sounded like Mick Jagger. Later, as I became familiar with (and used to) Jim's work, I saw a lot more differences between the two than similarities, but at first (because of the way the mind grasps for points of reference when confronted with something new) it was like he was a carbon copy. This seems strange to me now. In the case of the Femmes, my first reaction, especially to their first album, was that I'd never heard anyone who sounded so much like early Jonathan Richman and the Modern Lovers. No problem – I love that music and have always wished for more like it – but a month later the similarities are much less obvious to me. They're still there, I could probably point 'em out, but you see the more I become familiar with the Femmes' music the less they sound like anyone else and the more they sound like themselves. So much so, in fact, that they sort of exist out of time – I can imagine their three albums coming along and sounding weird, different, brilliant, at any point in the last fifteen years.

The Femmes, by the way, are not born-again Christians, despite what I read in *People* magazine. Gordon is a Baptist (his father's a Baptist minister in Milwaukee), and his church and his faith are very important to him (hence Violent Femmes songs like *Jesus Walking on the Water* and *Faith*), but he's not "born again" in that he never left his faith and his father's church is liberal, even radical from some perspectives, not the sort of fundamentalist outfit the "born again" label implies these days. Victor's a Catholic, and Brian's a skeptic—well actually I forgot to ask him, so I'm not sure, but he talks like one. Gordon doesn't seem to have a problem about being in a band with guys who don't share all his spiritual views; but he does definitely regard his music (and therefore the band's) as his pulpit, his opportunity to share his faith and spread the news to whoever out there might be ready to hear it. He has another band on the side, strictly gospel, called Mercy Seat, but fortunately he doesn't try to segregate the spiritual and the secular when he's with the Femmes. He mixes the two together in ways never quite attempted before (*Never Tell*, a song in which he threatens to cut up a female acquaintance if she rats on him—a scary, passionate, affecting performance, presumably he's projecting himself into another persona but he does it awfully convincingly—is followed on the *Hallowed Ground* album by *Jesus Walking on the Water*: "Oh my oh my oh my, what if it was true? ...Did he did he did he die on that cross, and did he did he did he come back across?"), and the results are every bit as successful as the many other odd musical and emotional and dramatic elements the Femmes mix together.

So no, I never took acid with Jim Morrison (we did fly across the country together once, and when we got to L.A. I asked him for the book of poetry I'd loaned him—David Henderson's *Felix of the Silent Forest*—and he didn't have it and seemed genuinely surprised when I made him go back on the plane to get it; it was like he'd already totally bought into the myth of his own powerlessness and irresponsibility), but I have been to church with Gordon Gano. It was the morning after the San Francisco concert, we drove to a small Baptist church in south Oakland that his father had recommended. It was great. There was a guest minister, a woman pastor from a church in Camden, New Jersey, and she was earthy, outspoken, outrageous and totally from the heart, a real ball of fire but not just in the classic black Baptist sense of putting on a good show. She entertained and got our attention, and then she used our attention as a channel for the truth, the spirit, which is just what rock and roll does at its best. Her talk was inspired, spontaneous, not that she didn't have some ideas of what she might do, just as a rock band has ideas of what songs they might play, but when she got to the pulpit she allowed the spirit to move through her, and then she used all her performing gifts to move her audience towards a place where the spirit could enter us. This requires real vulnerability, some kind of risk or sacrifice on the part of the participants, if it's purely ritual no authentic opening up occurs. Specifically, what I felt was an awareness of how my own anger at God and life shows up in day-to-day situations disguised as anger at the people I live or work with, or strangers, or myself—and how I lose my trust (and therefore my strength, and willingness to take risks) as a result. As I explain this it sounds very thought-out, intellectual, but of course it wasn't like that, like rock and roll this is a practical philosophy delivered and received on a visceral level, if it works it works not just as the emotions well up in church but two days later when you start getting frustrated about something and catch yourself feeling sorry for yourself. What I mean is, this minister was up to something more than carving notches in her Bible for each sinner that dramatically comes forward; she was committed to having more people experience the fruits of faith in their daily lives. Gordon and I were both deeply moved, and that night his performance of *Faith* (with inspired support from Peter Balestrieri and Sigmund Snopek as the Horns of Dilemma) drew the best audience response the song has ever gotten.

What with driving to church, and back to the hotel, and having lunch, and driving on to the gig in Santa Clara, I spent a lot of hours with Gordon Gano that day, and I'm sure if you've heard and been fascinated by his music you'll want to know, as I wanted to know, "what's he like?" I'm never quite sure how to answer this question. You can circle around it, as journalists do, with anecdotes and snippets of information about what the person wears and how he spends his time and what his friends say about him and so forth. But always I'm aware of an underlying pressure, maybe the unasked question beneath the vague catch-all of "what's he like?", which is the questioner's need to penetrate the mystery, to find out the nature of the power this other human, this songwriter or guitar player or actress or whoever it is, has over me, most of all to get closer to that person, just as sexual attraction compels us to get closer if we can.

The bottom line is always that the hero in question is a real person, with normal fears, doubts, bad habits, enthusiasms, hungers etc. This doesn't always make good journalism, because the illusion of "specialness" is what sells magazines and newspapers. The Femmes have a song called *Special* that plays with the positive and negative connotations of the word, pointing out that to be different can be attractive and can also be scary, and it'll turn around on you like that, a hard coin to spend.

The superficial mystery about Gordon Gano is here's this dirty-mouthed punk rocker who likes to go to church and is a devout Baptist, and also that he says "we don't want no killing" and yet sings songs full of murderous, angry imagery, delivered with a passion and conviction that the heavy metal bands seldom come near. This, as I say, is the surface level of mystery, which expresses itself in seeming contradictions and is quite baffling for people who aren't aware of all the contradictions that make up their own lives. A deeper lever is the artistic one: there's a movie called *Mystery of Picasso,* whose title refers, I think, to the mystery of Picasso's prodigious talent, his unique and inexplicable power, his hand moves and there's a line and then another line and he blots it all out and tosses another line on top and suddenly you're staring at a masterpiece. How? Where'd it come from? You're actually watching the paint hit the canvas, and you still don't know. As Gordon says, in *Heartache,* "Nobody ever taught you how to dance like that." Over and over in his songs he expresses awe at the sheer power (and danger) of a woman's beauty. The awe we feel at the artist, the songwriter, is the same thing. Might as well send an interviewer to write an article about what the beautiful girl who you saw at the dance last night is really like. What would you know if you knew? What would you have if you found out? Probably not her, but that is the illusion, and that's why we buy the magazine when our hero (or the object of our desire) is on the cover. I will tell you a few things about Gordon. He's charming, so much so that I think he has to work at turning it off, at being neutral, and so a lot of the time it's easier for him just to be alone. (He avoids hanging out with the band or anyone else any more than necessary while they're on the road, and this is a band that is on the road a lot.) He can sound sarcastic even when he doesn't intend to be; there were times in our conversation when he was relaxed and trusting and his words were unambiguous, but at other times his comments, like his songs, seemed impossible to nail down, you could take them a number of different ways. It's a gift, a power, a curse, maybe an automatic defense. (Now remember, I was this guy who's writing a book or something, he did have every reason to feel guarded.) The single most mysterious thing about Gordon, however — and as always I'm not really talking about the person, I'm talking about the person in the context of my expectations as a fan, someone who is interested in his art — is that the voice on the records is not the person I met. That is, I don't recognize it. I recognize the man I met in the words of his songs, the things he chooses to write about, the individualism of his material, his particular perspective on things, his fears and enthusiasms, it all seems to fit. But where did this voice come from, or rather, why didn't I meet this side of him? It sounds like some whole other person.

It's possible, though I don't know if it's true, that this is as much a mystery to Gordon (if he notices it at all, if this isn't just some weird quirk of mine) as it is to me. The artist doesn't necessarily know where the persona that's in his art comes from. (I'm not talking, by the way, about the personas in songs, like the guy in *Country Death Song,* but the recognizable voice that sings all those different parts, the presence who's playing the parts and doing the singing.)

I believe, however, that the key to the mystery has to do with the theatrical quality of the Violent Femmes' recordings and live shows, and also with that thing I saw when I was standing on stage at One Step Beyond, that wall of energy and attention so real you can almost reach out and touch it. There's a word that goes along with poet/philosopher/prophet, and the word is actor. The rock and roll philosopher works in a medium that combines music (which historically has always been closely linked to spiritual experience) with poetry and theater.

I have the impression from talking with Victor De-Lorenzo, the Femmes' drummer, who was an actor before he became a rock musician, that he works with Gordon in the recording studio on the vocal takes the way a director works with an actor: coaxing, guiding, suggesting. A few months ago Bob Dylan was interviewed by the Australian press, in a press conference that reads like it could have come from a Dylan tour in the mid-1960s. He was asked, "Who are you when you're not Bob Dylan?" and replied, "I'm only Bob Dylan when I have to be Bob Dylan... most of the time I can just be myself."

The follow-up question was, "How is your real self different?", and he answered, "Well, if you've got two minutes later I'll show you."

Among other things, this means that "real self" won't show up in a magazine profile (or a chapter in a book). By definition, if it's in a magazine or book or record or on stage, it's "Bob Dylan" or "Gordon Gano," the public image of whoever we're talking about. Doesn't matter if you catch the person sitting around in his socks just hanging out; when you describe the event in a book, the description becomes public and so it becomes part of the public myth, a subscript of myth called "what he's really like." It's not what he's really like, however.

It doesn't matter. We're not actually interested in the private person anyway (though we think we are), because that person isn't special. The specialness we're after comes when the performer, the artist, is on stage, or in front of a mike in a recording studio, or writing a song on a piece of paper, reacting to and creating with and for the attention field that he or she feels out there. There are instincts and awarenesses that operate in this environment that have little to do with any other moment in our lives.

To find out what he's really like, you'd have to be him as he's standing on that stage; and even then you wouldn't really know. You wouldn't know any more than what you can see and hear from the dance floor, standing out there in the audience.

The Doors' power when I saw them at Ondine in '66 or at the Fillmore East in '67 had something to do with who they were, but it had a lot to do with who their audiences were, as well. The excitement in the air didn't come from the band—it was just something an improvisational rock and roll band, particularly a band with a gift for musical drama and visual theater, could make good use of, playing the energy of the moment.

Playing in a rock and roll band is a great opportunity to get in touch with that energy, to find out what's happening in the world. Another opportunity that's open to all of us is to be part of the audience. Either way, the experience is one of giving and receiving. You may never know — you the performer or you the audience — who you've touched or how deeply. It doesn't matter. The work of poetry, prophecy, and philosophy is to share the truth. The work of music is spiritual healing. The work of theater is to let us see ourselves. Put the three together and you have heavy magic indeed, something worth traveling from town to town for, whether there's money and success in it or not.

The audience thinks, here comes another band. The band thinks, here comes another city. And then they meet in the night and dance.

Chapter Twelve

"No kinds of love/are better than others."
— The Velvet Underground

> Harmony, which has motions akin to the revolutions of
> our souls, is not regarded by the intelligent votary of the
> Muses as given by them with a view to irrational pleasure,
> which is deemed to be the purpose of it in our day, but as
> meant to correct any discord which may have arisen in the
> courses of the soul, and to be our ally in bringing her into
> harmony and agreement with herself; and rhythm too was
> given by them for the same reason, on account of the ir-
> regular and graceless ways which prevail among mankind
> generally, and to help us against them."
> — Plato

What the Sixties had that the Eighties don't have is
an illusion of community. Despite the quality, the
richness, the variety of rock and roll today, especially
live rock and roll, this absence is sorely felt. There is
something incomplete about even the best live shows.
The prevalence of people wearing t-shirts with bands'

names on them seems to me not so much a proclamation of identity as a plea for it. We hear ourselves in the music but when we look around we can't see ourselves in the crowd.

This loneliness is felt by the musicians as well. They can express their hearts and shout the truth so it bounces off the farthest walls, but what's missing is something bigger to be in service to. Some have found it for themselves, but only a very few — U2's Bono comes to mind — project a conviction that their audience is finding it too. I suppose Springsteen projected it and that's a big part of why he became so hugely popular. But the hunger he sensed and expressed has turned on him, I fear, so that regardless of his wishes in the matter he is now identified as the nourishment rather than the need. It's like you get out in front of the stampede and suddenly everyone thinks that maybe *you* are the mysterious It we've all been running after. Express the hunger and we'll make you king; become king and we'll eat you alive and complain that there wasn't more meat on your bones.

For a few brief years in the 1960s there was something like a collective illusion, a sense of working together in service to a real and imminent greater truth. We believed we were building something. That feeling was so satisfying that even today musicians and fans alike listen to the music that was made then and bemoan the loss of the intangible Something that made it all so special once. Why can't it be like that today?

The sad answer is, because the bubble burst, the magical sense of community came to naught and blew away, and it's hard to put an illusion back together again. The illusion of the Sixties was one of social transformation, a birth of new community from the ashes of the corrupt old order. The illusion was based on a very substantial (and, in hindsight, accurate) feeling of change taking place, old assumptions and old ways dying and new ways being born.

This did in fact occur, in many public and private realms of human perception and endeavor. But what failed to occur was the perpetuation of a sense of community and common purpose among those committed to ongoing transformation, revolution, personal and societal growth and change. The hippies, the peaceniks, the rock and rollers, the underground and the counterculture and their alternative media and lifestyles were all integrated back into the mainstream of society, and although the changes we spearheaded had a lasting impact, and touched more people than ever, the thrill of discovery, leadership, and danger was gone. The sense of belonging to a tribe of great adventurers, caught up in the momentum of a historic time of change, disappeared; and here we were belonging to nothing but society as a whole with all its inertia and corruption and purposelessness again.

Rock and roll became an institution, big business, it even took on a sort of bread-and-circuses quality, a diversion to keep youthful, revolutionary energy inside the stadiums and off the streets. Rock and roll stars by their actions promoted the use of alcohol, cocaine, heroin and other spiritually debilitating drugs, and along with Richard Nixon and the other role models of the day promulgated a value system in which winning, staying on top, and amassing large sums of money were the only things that really mattered.

Punk came along in the mid-late Seventies as a response to this, a revolution within the rock and roll ranks, and in many ways it was a successful revolution, the fruits of which are still very much with us today. Particularly musically, a kind of independence has been declared, and rock and roll's creative base has been significantly widened and revitalized.

The music is exciting again, there's a lot of different things happening and a plunge into the world of rock and roll in the mid-late 1980s can be extremely stimulating and rewarding. But good music does not in and of itself create community — at least, not the very powerful expanded and expanding sense of community we had for a few years in the 1960s.

The closest approximation of an illusion of community in the 1980s music scene can be found at a Grateful Dead concert. Not only are the superficial trappings there, such as the common symbology of skulls, roses, lightning bolts, but there is an authentic commonality as well, in the thoughts and feelings expressed in each show and the understanding and response of the audience. I was at a Dead concert yesterday that subtly, indirectly, and very powerfully made reference to the wounding of the earth that occurred in the Ukrainian nuclear disaster, and went on to remind us of the earth's strength and resilience and also of our need to participate in its care. And I know that consciously and unconsciously the message was felt and received by everyone there — indeed, the "message" comes not so much from conscious intention on the band's part as from the ability of their music to articulate the unconscious collective feelings of the people who are present.

At a good Dead performance everyone in the audience feels a sense of community, with each other and often with the human species as a whole, and in addition there is an actual community of Grateful Dead fans who live in different places but come together, barter, renew friendships, fall in love etc. at the shows. So there's real community, but there still isn't illusion of community in the particular sense I mean. For there to be illusion of community, as there was in the Sixties, the scene would have to be more expansive, there'd have to be other bands around working with the same kind of energy and something approaching a similar level of popularity. There'd have to be a sense and an experience of all of us being part of some larger movement, some great rising tide of the times.

This illusion of community I'm talking about has to be inclusive, it has to carry with it a feeling that the great day is coming when the whole world will get on board and be part of this — it can't be restricted to appreciation for a single band, one group of musicians. That's a personality cult, not a movement. These comments are not meant as a reflection on the Grateful Dead, who have been social and musical innovators for twenty-one years, and who contribute at least as much to earth music today as they did to San Francisco music in the Sixties, which is to say, a lot. They're a magnificent band. But even at a Dead concert it is possible to feel lonely, looking around and seeing all these people who don't even pretend to be committed to anything bigger than being at this show and maybe coming to the next one if they have the time and money. There is no real illusion generated that this beautiful day in the amphitheatre is part of a larger movement. It's just a Grateful Dead show, and it doesn't even hold out the promise of a world in which there are more Grateful Dead shows, since these boys are working about as hard as they possibly could be already.

Community may mean living together or liking the same band or going to the same church every Sunday. But "illusion of community" is a movement, like the anti-slavery movement of the nineteenth century or the peace, love, rock and roll and expanded consciousness movement of the late 1960s. Music takes on an extraordinary power during such moments of perceived common purpose and activity—it proclaims, amplifies, celebrates and unifies. The *I Ching* says, in describing the great sacrificial feasts and sacred rites of ancient China, "the sacred music and the splendor of the ceremonies aroused a strong tide of emotion that was shared by all hearts in unison, and that awakened a consciousness of the common origin of all creatures. In this way disunity was overcome and rigidity dissolved." That stands as an excellent description of the 1969 Woodstock Music Festival.

The danger for people of my generation (I turn 38 next week) and even for the generation that follows us is that we may be so attached to past glories—experienced firsthand or just heard tell of—that we miss the new and different glories of our present moment, as we stubbornly hold onto and hold out for the return of the-way-it-was-once. Ain't gonna return. Ain't gonna be another Beatles. Ain't gonna be another Woodstock. Might possibly be another all-encompassing illusion of community and common purpose, but if so it'll be different from the last one and anyway it's not the sort of phenomenon anyone can predict. What is for sure is that there's something even more important going on right now — by definition, because only what's happening now makes a difference.

What's happening now? Ten months into my journey, my rediscovery of rock and roll, what have I found? What message if any seems to be coming through the records I'm listening to and the shows I go to and the videos I watch?

The message I get is a personal one, but it has strong collective implications. It is that rock and roll is a resource, as much or more so today than it's ever been in the past. It is a healing music. It has a unique power to aid the individual listener in the process of locating himself or herself amidst the confusion and complexity of the modern world. In fact, the general purpose of rock and roll now is to allow people to discover and explore their own maps of personal and collective reality.

In a few months I'll be done writing this book about my own recent discoveries and explorations, but I can see already that my journey will continue, that in fact it's just beginning. The most satisfying thing I have learned about rock in these months is that it's not a shallow wilderness. The deeper I go into it the richer the scenery is, and the more paths there are to explore. "In wildness lies the preservation of the world" — I grew up with a normal twentieth century fear that there would be no wildness in my world or my children's world, no place for adventure, discovery, the unexpected, the unknown. When I got to college it felt like the end of the line, the end of youth, creativity, and freedom. None of the tricks I'd used in the past seemed to work any more — dramatics, school newspaper, foreign languages — and the future looked stultifying.

And then I got involved with the radio station, and started a rock and roll magazine...

And now, as my children become adolescents and I approach 40, the frontier has called me again, and the thing that amazes me is it's the same frontier I walked away from seventeen years ago because it was becoming too civilized. And I get out here and sure, there's dude ranches and shopping centers and whole bloody cities built on top of little settlements we established twenty years ago. But the territory as a whole has expanded so much that there's actually more wild country now than there was then, much more, and it seems like the more wonders I find the more there are left to discover. Rock and roll didn't grow up to fulfill the particular dreams I had for it; I guess I've been measuring it against those dreams in my mind all these years, and so I figured it hadn't grown up at all. But I was wrong...

> "The well is there for all. No one is forbidden to take water from it. No matter how many come, all find what they need, for the well is dependable. It has a spring and never runs dry."
>
> — The I Ching

Rock and roll exists outside of time, don't let my talk about the Sixties and the Eighties confuse you. The kids who listen to the Doors' first album or the Beach Boys' *Endless Summer* as though these records were made this year have got it exactly right. One of the disadvantages of the illusion of common purpose is that it naturally carries with it an illusion of progress. If rock and roll was part of this great collective effort towards some imminent and glorious new world, if the musicians and the audience were involved in an ongoing, evolving process of consciousness expansion, then we could and did expect each new record by the Beatles, the Stones, Bob Dylan et al to be better than the previous one, a news report on how far we'd gotten and where we were heading to next. A positive aspect of this was the way it fostered a kind of creative ambition and competition, the Stones and the Beatles always trying to top themselves and each other, of course it was ludicrous at times but it also did make them bolder, wilder, in a way it sustained that energy that we hear on a band's first record (*"this* will get their attention!"*) so that it kept going and kept building for six or seven years.

It was fun while it lasted, but it also left behind in me and probably a lot of other people a persistent illusion that this year's music is supposed to represent a moving forward from last year's music. To carry this kind of thinking to its logical conclusion, what's coming out now ought to be thirty or a hundred times better than *Maybellene* or *Milk Cow Blues,* and if it isn't, rock and roll has failed to grow.

The flaw in the logic is this: progress isn't growth. When you're a kid there are these marks on the kitchen wall that show how much taller you are now than six months ago and six months before that; but if you go back to that kitchen at age thirty-something hoping to find out how much more you've grown since you got out of high school, you're in for a disappointment.

Putting aside definitions of growth for the moment, my idea of a timeless model of rock and roll as a whole would be an enormous jukebox with selections arranged in no particular order. Any time you look at it there's old stuff, new stuff, records you love and records you can't stand, current favorites and classics you've forgotten about, and lots and lots of things you've never heard before, some of which are sure to turn out to be wonderful, powerful, written and sung and recorded just for you.

Any time you want you can reach over to the jukebox and punch up *Fun, Fun, Fun* by the Beach Boys and it'll sound like what rock and roll sounds like, and you can follow it with the Pretenders' *Middle of the Road* and Lisa-Lisa's *I Wonder If I Take You Home* and Bob Dylan's *Knocking on Heaven's Door* or any one of tens of thousands of other songs, album sides, videos, live performances (imaginary jukeboxes can play live performances, club, concert hall, or arena, your choice) and it'll just be glorious rock and roll coming at ya, if you like you can check the footnotes for history, dates, all kinds of neat information (like baseball statistics), but that's strictly optional, the music keeps playing regardless of history, in an order determined only by serendipity and the whims of your head and heart.

And if someone tries to sell you a program that tells you which songs are worth listening to and what order to play 'em in, don't buy it. Only the map you draw for yourself can possibly bring you home.

Chapter Thirteen

*"I can't even remember/if we were lovers/or if I just
wanted to..."*

— Violent Femmes

I remember standing at the back of the Unicorn, a
small club in Boston, in spring of 1967, watching Jefferson Airplane do a set. They were so tight and so free,
a rushing mountain stream of liquid music pouring
forth from Jack's bass, bright notes from Jorma's lead
guitar sparkling as in morning sunlight, Paul's rhythm
guitar adding intensity, fullness, commitment,
Spencer's drumming stretching to surround it all, sup-
porting, accepting, holding together, and Paul and
Marty and Grace's vocals rising, one atop the next,
soaring and diving and breaking free like waterbirds
feeding and playing in the stream of music; but what
most stands out in my memory are the electric glances
that went from Grace to Marty and Marty to Grace as
all of this exploded together and redoubled or quad-
rupled in power as they really took off on *It's No Secret*

or *The Other Side of This Life,* purity and strength and
joy and the fire of sheer hatred with all the negativity
taken out of it, just scream it out!, cascading off each
other and riding the music, riding each other, up, over,
around, through, a waterfall of guitars, voices, percussion splashing over the stage and all of us like we were
standing in it, behind it, and in front of it all at once. In
one sense I don't think they even knew we existed, and
in another sense they physically and actively loved each
one of us just for the fact of our being there, accepting,
receiving, inspiring their joy.

Bill Thompson, the Airplane's road manager, was
standing next to me, every bit as mesmerized and excited as I was. And I thought, here's a guy who watches
them do this twice a night, the same songs, month after
month, show after show, and he still can't get enough of
it, he's standing here like me, transfixed, hanging on
every note. I admired his power, to put himself in a
position to soak up so much spiritual energy, and to be
wise enough, innocent enough, free enough to keep
feeling the full passion of it, appreciating it, surrendering to it, letting it in. And I guess I was inspired by his
example, because for the next nine months or so I went
to see the Airplane night after night in New York, San
Francisco, Toronto, wherever they were that I could get
to, every chance I got.

A gal I knew went to a Patti Smith Group gig in the
spring of '75 and ended up travelling to every show they
did anywhere in the northeast for the next five or six
months. I was almost like that with Springsteen in '74-
'75, and I was far from alone—there was a gang of
people, some from the music biz and some totally unrelated to it, who'd be there show after show after show.

And if you'd caught one of those shows, you'd know why. Coming out of Yoko Ono's concert the other night I saw a woman in a Translator jersey whom I'd seen standing near the front of the crowd a few nights earlier when Hüsker Dü played the Fillmore, who'd also been at at least the last three or four Translator shows I was at. Translator has a hard core of fans in the Bay Area who come to virtually every show, there's one bunch of 'em who live way out in Chico or somewhere and drive hundreds of miles to get to the shows, and I know the guys in Translator feel like it's the support and love of these fans that's kept them going when everything else (except the music) seemed to be against them. And from the fans' point of view, Translator supports *them* and keeps their spirit renewed by coming through, creating miracles of musical improvisation and unpretentious, heartfelt communication, night after night. Their friends think they're crazy (the fans' friends, probably Translator's friends too), but it doesn't matter — it's just so satisfying to discover how much energy and commitment and caring you're able to put out when you truly find somebody to love.

I went backstage after another exceptional Translator performance at Berkeley Square last fall, and told the band how great it had been, and Steve said, "How could we do any less with all that love coming at us?" And, maybe because Translator's last encore had been a Beatles' song, I suddenly had a picture of the Beatles standing on stage in the Cavern in Liverpool in 1962, feeling all the love coming at them from their passionately loyal fans, and responding with something a little better than the very best they could do, transcending limits, the energy building on itself until performers and audience were in this uncharted territory where no one had ever gone before.

That kind of love is a source of power; I'm sure it played a big part in making the Beatles ready to go out from Liverpool and conquer the world.

We as audience, and we as performers, have one message that we repeat over and over again, it's completely timeless and the Beatles said it just about perfectly: "please please me, oh yeah, like I please you." When Translator sings "edge of the sea, edge of the sand, edge of the future in the edge of our hand," I hear the same message—something about the need for love bringing us into the moment and how being here together in the moment we feel the presence of and responsibility for and excitement of what will be.

To create consciously, to love honestly, we have to feel the excitement and the responsibility both at once. In this respect, one of rock and roll's jobs could be to sell us the future, to sell us on the value (in spite of the pain) of being alive and awake, to show us how exciting and fulfilling it can be, to tempt us, as it were, into choosing life. (Sexual attraction does a similar job in a similarly crude and subtle fashion.) But this cannot be done through a pollyanna approach, trumpeting the good stuff and ignoring or covering up what's unpleasant. Rock and roll generally takes another tack, that of acknowledging pain, anger, self-pity, injustice, fear, getting down to the dark and hidden stuff and embracing it, shouting about it, acknowledging its presence and welcoming its truth and thus releasing us from the pressure of what can't be looked at or said.

Donna points out that another Translator phrase, "It's all right to feel what you feel" (from a song called

Friends of the Future), seems to be the basic statement rock and roll is making and has always made. I agree, and it mostly does this not at a distance, as in assuring you it's all right, but in a participatory fashion: you hear your own anger, fear, desire, self-doubt expressed in a song (the words, the beat, the sound, the loudness, or everything together) and you immediately feel less alone and probably start shouting along with it. It must be all right to feel this if someone else feels it and is willing to say it, sing about it, publicly; and it isn't buried inside you any more when you're shouting it at the top of your lungs.

Now to some extent the situation I'm describing is an ideal. Most rock and roll fans and critics, like most people anywhere, won't acknowledge the "like I please you" part; they're passive, they want to be pleased, period, and they figure they did their part when they paid their money at the door. And the band may try to go along with this, try hard to please 'em and give 'em a good show for their money, but it's not gonna work very well, there's just a natural limit to how much you can feel when you're not actively participating in the experience, or put it another way, love's much more profound when you're giving and getting at the same time. There is such a thing as one-sided love, I guess, but you can't create the future with it.

Hüsker Dü's new album *Candy Apple Grey* opens with a sound that might be crystal shattering (the first song is called *Crystal*), followed by a rapid drumbeat and then a frantic guitar-and-bass riff and, ten seconds later, a shrill, hoarse vocal sung so fast with so much noise around it you're surprised you can actually hear some of what he's saying, something about "a thousand

miles an hour" and then the start of the chorus: "time
to let off some pressure/time to let off some steam..." If
it sounds like I'm describing a standard issue heavy
metal album for frustrated male teenagers
("headbangers") then I'm not doing it justice — put on
Hüsker Dü and nine out of ten heavy metal fans will
rush in from the next room shouting, "What is that
awful noise? Christ, turn it off!" At this point your best
tactic is to turn it down and appeal to the macho instincts of your (younger brother, older sister, parent,
child, roommate) by explaining that it's Hüsker Dü
from Minneapolis — home of Prince, Bob Dylan, the
Replacements — who set out five years ago to be the
loudest, fastest punk band in the world, live and on
record, and succeeded. If you're lucky the piercing brilliant intensity of *Crystal* will be over by this time, and
while you distract the person with the inner sleeve lyric
sheet — "we're talking about two of the best songwriters
in the world today, look at these words!" — his or her
subconscious mind will be seduced by the gorgeous
melodic hook of *Don't Want to Know If You Are Lonely*
and you can get away with playing the record a few
times in a row, by which point your friend is shouting
along to *Sorry Somehow* and wondering if you've got
any more albums by these Husker guys. That's the best
case scenario — there's also a good chance you'll have
the record broken over your head.

The mere fact that you're reading this book does not
oblige you to listen to or like Hüsker Dü, so relax. But
the role this record plays in my own rock journey is an
interesting one. I bought their previous album a few
months ago and it didn't appeal to me much, I played it
a number of times, pushing myself because it came so

highly recommended, but although a couple of the songs started to grow on me the overall sound was just too frenetic, it jangled me and I didn't like that feeling so I let it go, still curious about why people rave about this band but deciding it was just one of the many types of rock music that aren't my cup of tea, just like I've never doubted the brilliance of Robert Fripp, say, but have never gotten into his records either. There's so much out there, if you tried to expose yourself to everything, or to like everything your friends want you to like, you'd go nuts. I mean, it's okay to be missing out on something great (though it can hurt, in retrospect; I think of the many times I passed up opportunities to see Bob Marley & the Wailers in their early days), as long as you're getting what you need from what you are listening to.

And then Bill Graham Presents booked Hüsker Dü into the Fillmore, heading a bill with two other bands I've also been curious about (Faith No More, who were a real disappointment live, and Camper van Beethoven, who were delightful), and I just had to go check it out, and by way of getting maximum value out of the experience I bought the brand new HD album, and spent an afternoon before the show playing each side four or five times in a row, with increasing pleasure and fascination.

I was impressed by Hüsker Dü live, I enjoyed myself, I was glad I went, but I didn't really get that excited, a nice nonstop blur of fast loud music, extraordinary amount of noise from just three guys (like Cream or Hendrix), I liked their unstylish appearance and general attitude but I wouldn't follow 'em around from show to show like I do Translator or like I would Green on Red or the Violent Femmes given half a chance. The main thing about their live show is it made me feel more connected to them — I know what they look like, I have a sense of them as human beings — and it gave me a reason to expose myself to *Candy Apple Grey* despite my difficulties with *Flip Your Wig*. And *Candy Apple Grey* is a great record. Their music still jangles me, but in this case it's worth it, because this is the most satisfying record in my house right now, I'm not sure what need it fills for me but it's a deep one.

Mystery. It's just natural for me as a writer and talker to get into this mode where I'm trying to explain everything, and it's bullshit, I have to stop myself. I have to slap myself and remember that I'm an idiot. Turn towards the mystery. The rest of it, the part that can be explained, doesn't matter. It's the stuff I don't understand, the paths I haven't walked on yet, that draw me forward. Edge of the future. *Candy Apple Grey* challenges me, superficially because of its loudness and speediness but that's just the surface. The real challenge is its beauty. That's terrifying. A deeper layer of my onion is being peeled away, ugly crawling things under a log, I don't want to look but the truth is I do want to, I need to, and it's exciting as well as scary. Mystery. Beauty. Set me free.

Ugly shouldn't be this beautiful. This stop was not on my itinerary. I don't know what I'm doing here. Help! (And I hear these voices telling me, "Relax, you're okay, everything's going to be all right," and that scares me even more.)

Here's something I wrote ten or eleven years ago, part of an article about Neil Young:

"I hope you saw Bob Dylan singing *Hurricane* on television (the salute to John Hammond) – he was very good. You couldn't see that performance – I *hope* you couldn't – without feeling and thinking about the *strength* of the man, isn't it incredible, what is it, where does it come from, how does it contribute to or relate to his work?

"Every time I see that strength (it has been my good fortune to see it more than once over the years, in Dylan, in Neil Young, in Phil Dick and others) and feel the greatness of the music or art that goes with it, I am forced once again to confront the realization that strength in the Emersonian sense (to thine own self be true) is the absolute prerequisite of artistic greatness, God-given talent is nothing without the stamina and the will to use that talent again and again in the face of all odds, in the face of doubts and terrors that other people (those who don't make superhuman efforts of will over and over) can never imagine nor hope to experience.

"To me, a great artist is someone who says 'I am' more honestly, more powerfully, more beautifully, more straightforwardly, more inclusively than anyone else except other great artists. This is not a yardstick I use to judge people or their works; rather, it is a hypothesis I've been forced to consider after years of reading and looking and listening and saying, 'Hey, that's great!' and then wondering why...especially wondering why certain people can do it again and again, without really repeating themselves. Why are they great? What are they doing that's different?

"My answer, my deduction, my hypothesis is: they are being themselves more completely. That's all."

Rock and roll tempts me to be more of myself, and it does more: it guides me to soft spots, openings in myself, that I might never have found otherwise, or that I might have had to search for for years and years. (I don't mean it allows me to seal these openings, just the opposite — it opens them wider, lances the boil, breaks the shell, and allows the beginning of real growth and healing.)

It is (it has become again, since I resubmitted myself to its discipline) a kind of oracle for me, a truthsayer, direct line to a higher wisdom. Another oracle I use is the *I Ching*, the ancient Chinese "book of changes," and one reason that book has served me so well over the years is it speaks to me authoritatively without the intercession of another human being, there's no one there for me to argue with, to use my "word power" on. I can listen or refuse to listen, accept or refuse to accept, and that's all.

Rock and roll works for me in a similar fashion, and while its guidance is usually less specific than the *I Ching*'s, it has a greater ability to bypass my mental process and speak directly to my feelings, my heart. Rock and roll touches me in places my mind is unaware of, afraid of, even places where my mind is forbidden to go. It is my shortcut to the unknowable inside me.

This works through the power of attraction, a kind of seduction. My self-image didn't want to have anything to do with Tears for Fears, but *Shout* got to me anyway, and forced itself and the rest of their music (especially *The Hurting*) into my life. Hüsker Dü's music repelled me at first, and I pushed it away; it still makes me uncomfortable, but the beauty I've started hearing in it is so profound I can't doubt or deny that this stuff is meant for me, fills needs I didn't even know I had. As a matter of fact I'm in love with *Candy Apple Grey*, and this shocks me. What do I want with all this discord, anguish, depression, and pain? I want to say I don't need it, but I can't, because listening to the record has taught me different. I feel like an open wound today; but I also feel bigger, more whole, than I ever have before.

The discipline in my relationship with rock and roll works something like this: I have to keep letting go of my ideas and structures, what's good and what's bad, what I like, what's hip and all that stuff, and stay in touch with the part of me that is dissatisfied, that is hungry, that is unfulfilled. It also has to do with deciding that there's something here for me, and holding to that decision precisely at those moments when I feel the most doubt, when there's the most evidence in the other direction. If I had a lesser degree of commitment, I would almost certainly drop out of my search before I got down to whatever it is that's calling me. Indeed, it is a normal pattern in human life that the greatest desire to turn away from the path comes just before the moment of breakthrough.

I have been drawn back into rock and roll in such an active way, I suspect, not because there's more good new music now than there's been for a while, although that might be true, but because I need what this discipline, this intense commitment to and involvement in rock, has to offer me personally at this moment in my life and growth.

I have a problem with my compact disc player. I love it but I don't listen to it very much. Partly the problem is financial — I can't afford to buy an amp and speakers to go with it (my phonograph is a cheap, self-contained system with no input holes) and so I hook up the CD player to a boom box, not exactly a high-tech approach. Also, CDs cost so much – I bought quite a few of them while in the throes of my early infatuation with the device, but still my selection is narrow compared to my records and tapes, especially because these days I'm finding myself mostly interested in new music. A lot of the new music I'm listening to isn't available on CD, and also when I take a risk on something new I'm more likely to risk $7 on an lp than $14 on a compact disc. So a lot of what I've bought for the CD player is tried-and-true favorites, but it turns out that old favorites aren't my meat this year, I'm hungry for new experiences, revelations, the unexpected.

In a way I'd hoped the CD player itself would be a revelation, I had visions of myself hearing all the music I've loved over the years as if it were brand new, as if I were hearing it in a recording studio from the master tape, blasting over these big speakers, each new tune sounding like the best thing that ever happened to me. And I did get a taste of that, the night after I bought my Sony portable in New York, Ed Stasium brought his CDs of *Electric Ladyland* and *Who's Next* and *Beggar's Banquet* and *Highway 61 Revisited* down to the studio and the Translator guys and I took turns listening on headphones, it was incredible.

But since then – I like the convenience of the CD player, you don't have to turn the record over, some of my discs (Dylan's *Biograph*, Motown's songwriter collections, Creedence's *Chronicle*) are an hour long, it's great to put on before going to bed or something. But my dreams of rediscovering rock and roll, opening up sonic realms I've always dreamed of but never could get to before (you know, you want to turn the song up even louder but it starts distorting so bad you have to hold back, sidetracked on the road to heaven), that hasn't quite happened. Obviously my expectations for the CD player were unrealistically high, my problem is I was hoping for miracles, not just once or twice but every time I turn the thing on, and of course I was disappointed.

Video rock is kind of a similar story — I'm limited by my financial position (no cable, no VCR) and also by the economics of a new medium: the videos I'd like to see are by acts like Los Lobos, Lone Justice, Violent Femmes, U2, R.E.M., Jesus & Mary Chain and so forth, and most of these groups aren't popular enough to be in heavy rotation on MTV or to have videocassette compilations available at my local rental store. But just as with the CDs, these are limitations I could overcome if I wanted to bad enough — some of the San Francisco dance clubs have great selections of "new music" videos, for example. The real problem is that the videos I've seen and the CDs I've heard have not yet made me feel that there's something out there for me, something so wonderful that it's worth whatever commitment I have to make to be part of this.

Commitment needs inspiration. In order to watch music television all I have to do is go over to my friend's house less than a mile from here — to watch rock videocassettes I do the same thing, with a stop at the nearby video store first, $3 a rental ain't much — but what I find is I don't get around to it very often. By contrast, to go to a live concert or club date I have to drive to the city, an hour or more in each direction, and yet I find myself quite willing to go to two or three shows a week. This doesn't represent a conscious determination on my part that live rock is a more significant part of the current scene than video rock. Rather it's a choice my heart is making almost in spite of the ideas my mind has about where I "should" put my attention.

The records I've been buying inspire me more than the compact discs I've carefully selected, so I find myself spending most of my listening time with records. The live shows I've been to inspire me to the point where I keep committing myself to more, despite the long, late-night drives, the noisy, crowded, smoke-filled rooms, the frequent disappointments (saw the Replacements at the Fillmore, I was expecting great things but they were drunk and disinterested, who needs this?), and despite the fact that I have no real companionship at most of these shows and I've long since satisfied my curiosity about who the audiences are and what it's like. The music itself, my experience with it, is drawing me back — I didn't plan it this way, but I'm finding something I need out there, and so the commitment it takes to get tickets and drive to the shows and so forth comes naturally, my hunger directs me, this is where my heart wants me to be.

Rock and roll should be exciting. The idea that rock isn't exciting anymore could certainly keep a person from exposing himself or herself to today's rock recordings and performances, but if he gets past that and does hear something that truly excites him, no idea or position or mental attitude is going to stop him from coming back for more. This is the power of the music, that it can bypass the mind and connect directly with people's souls.

Addictive drugs can do the same thing. And I suppose for some listeners rock and roll is nothing more than an addiction, a parasite that obstructs growth instead of encouraging it, a place for the soul to hide. This is hard for me to imagine, however, because my own experience of rock is so different—I've gotten bored with it at times, lost interest, but at the times when it has been important to me it has never let me rest, has always goaded me on towards greater knowledge of myself and others, has always pushed me away from comfort and automatic behavior and pushed me towards challenge, awakening, mystery. Rock and roll has never been a safe space for me, it has always been a releaser of dark forces: sexuality, anger, God-intoxication, tribalism, hunger, and fear. It has always functioned as a red-hot rocket ride out of comfort, familiarity, and security and into danger, passion, the unknown, creativity, and unreasonable, irrational joy.

Turn towards the mystery. That is my commitment to myself, and rock and roll provides me a wild, anarchic discipline by being such a fountain of mystery, such a reliable source of the unpredictable and the unexpected. There's something here for me, there always has been and probably always will be, and the variable is my hunger, my willingness to immerse myself, my ability to let go, and scream, and hate, and dance, and love. It may sound like a mighty easy discipline, but don't you believe it. It takes a lot of courage to keep drinking from this fountain. It would feel a lot safer to stay home, and drink bottled water, and dream of mysteries gone by.

Chapter Fourteen

"Tonight we'll build a bridge/across the sea and land."

—U2

Senate hearings on rock lyrics. The issue was, graphic references to sex, violence, and drug use in rock and roll albums parents found their teenagers and even subteens listening to (i.e., almost every song on almost every heavy metal record, and *Darling Nikki* on Prince's ten-million-selling *Purple Rain*). It was a big deal last fall when I started on this book—magazine and newspaper articles all the time, lots of bombast on both sides, save our children versus save our freedom of speech. Now it's ancient history—didn't this exact same thing go on when Elvis first became popular, in 1956?—at least, until the next time these sacred American principles clash: the Freedom to Make Money versus the Freedom to Make Political Hay. I guess it would be too bad for the big record companies if they couldn't sell heavy metal to teenagers in shopping malls, and the independent record companies and stores starting getting all that business, and it would also be too bad for the musicians and fans if that meant the record guys started getting pushier about what you can and can't say on your record, but rock and roll survives, and anyway the deal's already been cut, Political Hay got theirs and Money's back to business as usual. So it goes with most issues of rock politics, or at any rate the visible ones: the deal goes down.

Another example of rock politics, fringe righteousness department: some punk fans (and punk rock writers) won't even listen to the new Hüsker Dü album because it's released through Warner Brothers instead of on an independent label. Obviously, the issue isn't independence at all (the music on the album is fiercely individualistic), but symbols of independence. Flag-waving turns up everywhere.

The surface politics of rock has been of less interest to me on this rock and roll journey than I thought it would be. I started out reading a lot of articles, I tried to identify and distinguish the different rock audiences I saw at the shows, but pretty soon I got caught up in the music and that other stuff didn't seem to matter. I had to put aside my agenda and follow my instincts instead. It was like I had to choose between an objective, orderly, broad-based representation of the rock experience, or a subjective, chaotic, narrow one, and I discovered I really had no choice: I couldn't tell the objective truth because there isn't any, it doesn't exist. Rock and roll is a wholly subjective experience.

Chuck Berry could tell you what rock and roll is, and so could Jimi Hendrix, or John Lennon, or Gordon Gano. But no two of them would tell you the same thing. I like this comment by Michael Steele of the

Bangles, quoted in *People* magazine: "We're just reinterpreting sounds. The Beatles interpreted Chuck Berry and Buddy Holly. It's a never-ending process. Basically it's all modern folk music, passed down through generations." That's true. And you don't even have to pick up a guitar to interpret your favorite rock sound—you do it every time you listen to a record or a song in a show, you do it with your ears, with your feelings, with your mind and with your whole body, and you do it differently each time. And the sum of all those private interpretations is what you think rock and roll is, and you're right. Every fan has his or her own private Rock and Roll Hall of Fame, and that's how it should be, I believe; institutions, standards and generalizations work contrary to the forces that give rock and roll its power.

Is rock and roll now an agent of change? It can be. It depends very much on what the performer wants and what the individual listener wants. Sometimes we think we want change but in fact we only want the feeling of it, the release, an exciting night of rebellion and then back to the same bleak reassuring familiarity in the morning. Heavy metal is a music of ritualized barrier-smashing, in which the icons of rock and roll—the guitar solo, the scream, the riff, the superficial outrage—are elevated to the status of high theater, an opportunity for a frenzied, ecstatic release of aggression, break down the walls, but they're always only prop walls within a larger, untouchable, immovable prison. It's an opportunity for those who perceive themselves as powerless to have an experience of power, without actually taking any risks.

When I was seventeen I loved the Yardbirds for the exact same musical and visceral reasons that teenagers today love the Scorpions or Metallica or Motley Crüe or AC/DC – indeed it was almost the same music, heavy loud blues-based kinetic rock and roll, slashing guitars, hot solos, crashing drums. The difference if any was that the Yardbirds didn't know what they were doing, it was an experiment, a process of discovery. When they did stumble into something big they barely recognized it, moved on to try something else, and left it to their successors to refine the sound and the style and make fortunes, make history.

Today most heavy metal bands know exactly what they're doing – some do it better than others, but still the rules of the form have been established, they can be stretched in many directions (Van Halen has been particularly clever) but they cannot be violated. This is not a music of hope, and in no way is it a music of real freedom, because it firmly rejects the possibility of actual change. Women are ritualistically trampled on in the lyrics because the male musicians and fans feel frustrated by the power women have to dominate them; but a world in which that domination did not occur would be a world in which there would be no satisfaction in striking back, and much worse, a world in which a man would be responsible for his own life and decisions. Female fans similarly enjoy both the pedestal they're placed on and the ritualized degradation, because in both cases it promises security. In sadomasochism, the essential truth is that both parties are dominated; neither has nor desires freedom. Heavy metal is a music that resonates with those who feel powerless, dominated – it allows them the experience of responding to, reacting against, triumphing over and even annihilating the oppressor, without threatening them with any possibility of actual confrontation or real change.

I suspect that for many people today heavy metal is an exciting way station on their rock and roll journey, a place where much of the power and joy of the music can be found, but that gets left behind when the heart starts asking for more and deeper and discovers all it's ever offered is more of the same. At this point some fans may move away from rock and roll altogether, or retreat into pop music and radio's generic "album rock," or continue to hold the excitement of heavy metal in a sort of nostalgic regard while no longer really participating. Some will stay true to heavy metal forever. And some will go on to seek elsewhere in the rock universe the kind of passion and commitment that heavy metal expressed for them until they exhausted it. This last group are the people who wish rock and roll to be, and therefore allow it to be, a personal and collective agent of change.

Every genre of rock and roll, not just heavy metal, produces a certain proportion of committed fans who expand beyond their original interests to go looking for whatever they can find anywhere in the music, past and present (but with an emphasis on present, I think; the past is too easy a place to hide), that will offer them something alive and unexpected, something to which they can give in return. In this way rock and roll encourages self-awareness and supports and stimulates personal growth. What the listener offers in return is his or her time and attention, the most sincere gifts anyone can give.

I notice I've made a lot of generalizations, about heavy metal in particular, even though I just finished saying that generalizations work against what gives rock and roll its power. My generalizations may be useful in that they illustrate the kind of thoughts I have about how rock and roll now is and isn't an agent of change. But taken at face value, they could also be distorting and destructive, so what I ask you to remember is, I don't know what I'm talking about.

This is true. I know very little about heavy metal. For that matter, by the standards of a true fan, I also know very little about Hüsker Dü, and only a moderate amount about U2, Springsteen, the Grateful Dead. Not that knowledge is so important — but the destructive quality of generalizations comes from the illusion on the part of those who hear 'em that they're based on knowledge. They're not — and this applies even to history, science, philosophy. Generalizations are always an intuitive leap (sometimes accurate, sometimes pure hogwash), and what they're based on, in a word, is attitudes. Obviously I have an attitude about heavy metal. But if that makes you think I know something, that would be too bad, because it could get in the way of your willingness to go and check out the scene yourself. Expose a person to enough generalizations, enough negative attitudes, and he'd never feel like checking out anything that's happening out there, and that I believe is exactly what kept me and what's kept most of us from experiencing the richness and variety of present-day rock and roll.

But look at what you miss when you hide out in your doubts and disbeliefs! Yesterday I experienced a miracle, the sort of rock and roll moment that will live in my memory forever, like my experiences years ago with the Airplane and the Doors. (Or the time I rode from Boston to New York, on a freezing November day in '66, on the back of Nick Peck's motorcycle, to see B.B. King and Bobby Blue Bland at the Apollo.) It was like something I'd been wishing for but not even believing was possible, and suddenly there it was, without warning or any planning or anticipation on my part, totally spontaneous, a gift from the universe.

I was in Berkeley and I just happened to buy a newspaper, for the silliest of reasons: on Fridays the *San Francisco Examiner* runs next week's top ten list (singles and albums) from *Billboard*, and I guess I'm still an eleven-year-old at heart, I wanna see the positions. And then I checked the entertainment column and saw this item:

> **Hot Notes**: Hottest note of the week came and went quickly — sales of tickets for a hastily arranged Prince concert (tonight at the Warfield Theatre) were announced on a dozen radio stations Wednesday afternoon and sold out minutes later.

I hadn't heard about this, not being much of a radio listener. Fortunately it was still mid-afternoon. I called the woman at Bill Graham's office who has been helping me get tickets to local shows while I work on this book, and asked if there was any way... She and her associate very kindly turned up a ticket for me, and at eight p.m. I was walking into the Warfield, one of two thousand amazed and excited people (this was the only San Francisco Prince concert this year, and we were going to see him and the Revolution in a 2200-seat theater instead of the 15,000-seat Cow Palace, which he easily sold out five nights in a row in '85).

I should add that of all the people and groups currently performing – with the exception of Bob Dylan and U2, both of whom are coming to town next month – Prince is the act I most wanted to see this year. I missed his shows last year, although I was already a big fan, just because it didn't enter my head to try to get tickets to any kind of concert then. (I might have thought of it in passing, but I quickly let other considerations be more important – time, money, effort, conflicting responsibilities.) And then last week he made a surprise appearance at the Bangles' Warfield concert, playing guitar on *Manic Monday* and returning for an encore later with *Whole Lotta Shakin' Going On*. I consider Prince one of the greatest innovators and overall talents on the rock and roll scene in the 1980s, and his presence during those brief moments with the Bangles was so powerful, so playful, so moving, I decided right then to do whatever I had to do to see one of his shows this summer. It happened sooner than I expected!

And what a show. It made the live videotape of his '85 show seem ten years old, he and the band have matured so much in the meantime. His dancing, his singing, Wendy's guitar-playing and stage presence (and indeed everyone in the Revolution was spectacular), his arrangements, his patter, his timing, his love of music and his awareness of its power, his joy in performing – it was like he'd been listening to Sam Cooke's *Live at the Harlem Square Club* album and reading Peter Guralnick's great liner notes and he decided to do his best to bring "uptown" to the masses. "Tonight you're mine," he told us; "tonight your name is Uptown." And he pulled it off, even with a 95% white audience – and he did it with dignity, with abandon, with humor, with glorious musicianship... Words fail me. All I know is, this is what it's all about. If his next set of arena shows can come even halfway close to what he did at the Warfield, they'll be unforgettable.

Music is constantly pressing forward. U2's The Edge, in a moving documentary about the making of their *Unforgettable Fire* album (available on videocassette), speaks of the band as being in service to the music, not creating it so much as letting it through. I just watched *Monterey Pop* again, for the first time in years, and it's such a great portrait of that moment in time – specifically and paradoxically because performances like Janis Joplin's *Ball and Chain* and Otis Redding's *I've Been Loving You Too Long* are so timeless, nothing in their style or content ties them to a particular era, and so what comes through is how the energy of the moment can make a space, a platform, where timeless greatness can and must occur. Janis seems a scared child who is only able to open her mouth because of the incredible loving support she's getting from her band and from the audience and from the rising energy of the scene, and then when she opens it what extraordinary courage tumbles out, what an amazing awareness of the drama of life and love and song, trailblazing, like those never-heard-before notes and changes from Jimi Hendrix's guitar (on *Wild Thing* – his voice does some trailblazing too) that seems to be playing itself as he waves his hand over it, the magician.

It was a moment for magicians. If this isn't another one, what was that Prince concert – or the Green on Red show I saw at Berkeley Square last month, or Lone Justice at the Stone – all about? I think the music wants to tell us something. It presses forward, it comes through, it reasserts our humanity and the depth and power of the possibilities open to us even as we falter and hesitate and dissemble and generally try to reassure ourselves that there's no hope and nothing's happening and we won't be fooled again. I mean, nuclear winter's not such an attractive outlook, but at times I think we find it less threatening than the embarrassment of taking part in another false dawn. But the music keeps tempting us to come out and play anyway...

I went to another Rush concert, this time an outdoors one, at Sacramento's Cal Expo Amphitheater. I had no difficulty enjoying myself this time. What a remarkable band they are! They fly in the face of all the rules — in my case, my preference for live music to be improvisational (it's funny, every band I talk to...the Grateful Dead, Translator, the Violent Femmes...has at some point expressed the belief that they're the only ones who play improvisational live rock any more; not true, fortunately). Rush does their whole show according to strict prearrangement (guitarist Alex Lifeson was asked in a *Guitar Player* interview, "Do you ever take chances onstage and play something you haven't tried before?" His answer was, "No. We're so regimented in all our parts, and we depend on each other for cues for the next parts. If somebody does one thing different, it could screw up somebody else's part. So we just stay away from that"), and yet the show vibrates with immediacy, they definitely put love and care and everything they're feeling at the moment into every note.

"When I know this song, I'm gonna like it." Donna's five-year-old Erik made this comment one day while we were playing a game and listening to a Translator album. The song was *Breathless Agony*, but of course the comment has universal applications. I said earlier that if there's a revolution taking place in rock and roll, it's a revolution of attitudes, and a revolution led and carried out by listeners rather than musicians. Whether or not a new illusion of community comes into existence may be out of our hands, but there is no question in my mind that the time has come for us to let go of our illusions of separateness, all the boring dead-end categories of rock, the belief that there are all these different audiences, and all the ideas in our heads about what we like and don't like (categorically) and what it looks like when rock music is doing what it's supposed to do.

Excess baggage. There are new truths that can't be read through the old lenses. If you or I want to use present-day rock and roll as a map towards the treasure of personal and collective identity, the only key we need is an open heart, which means a willingness to listen to that little voice inside saying, "when I know this song, I'm gonna like it." Nothing else could have brought Rush or Prince or Hüsker Dü or Translator or the Violent Femmes into my life. And the only action needed to let go of the illusion of separateness is to know and trust that others hear the same voice. They may hear it at different times, for different songs; and they may or may not be ready to listen to it. But they hear it, and that means I'm wrong when I see them as firmly locked into some other reality that will never intersect with mine. How do I know?

The power of rock is that it is inclusive rather than exclusive. Anyone can play. But that alone would be too easy. The rest of the story is, it demands participation.

It can help create community, it can help with whatever there is to create, because it requires response, it calls to life, it refuses to solace the passive, it says, "Get up and dance!" It forgives and loves but will not let us rest. It is an open door and a kick in the pants, and the day it stops being these things its star will have faded and its era will be past. That day has not yet come.

I'm feeling a little sad about Translator, because the news I hear is that the record isn't selling, they're on the road and there's not much attendance at the shows, maybe 50 people a night in most places, and one of the members plans to leave the band at the end of the tour. I don't think Translator will break up, but I don't know. I hope they won't, though no one could blame them – at this point the stresses are enormous.

I'm sad because I know these guys and love them and they deserve better, and when their music isn't being heard it's a loss for all the rest of us, especially for those who are hungry for this music and would love it and don't even know it's there. It's tempting to make a scapegoat of the record company for being so unsupportive, but that's the low road, and I believe in the end we create our own fates regardless of what others do to us or don't do for us. Or perhaps it would ease my pain to romanticize Translator's plight, but I don't like that path either.

The simple truth is, success and failure are not accurate barometers of inner worth, and sometimes the road's a rocky one. You can't always get what you want. And the deeper truth is, what's yours cannot be taken away from you, and this is true for both the creators and the receivers (who create by taking it in). I know all sorts of neat stories of how things have worked out magically for Translator in the last six months, little miracles on stage and in the recording studio and elsewhere, like how the album ended up with that beautiful, perfect cover photograph by Bob. It's natural to feel cheated when it seems that all the magic isn't adding up to what you, what I, thought it would lead to—but it's also great foolishness, how do I know what will be or what needs to be?

So the process goes on, they're playing their tour (and my sources tell me the music is great, it keeps coming through and the people who hear it are loving it), and worrying about the future like we all do, and I'm feeling a little sad, and you know if tomorrow it was the big surprise hit single and we were all feeling ecstatic, that would be great but it wouldn't necessarily mean that they'd have more impact then or that they're having less impact now.

I guess it's a matter of faith with me that we do what we're here to do, with love and dedication, and in doing so we touch the people we're meant to touch and have as much impact as any human can possibly have, and what it looks like from outside doesn't matter. Am I romanticizing it now? I don't know, sometimes the myth of the rock and roll band really bores me. I don't believe the world's a better place because U2 sells millions of records; I believe it's a better place because U2 exists and keeps making music, and if they stop making music it will be a better place because of the music they did make, and quantitative measurements don't affect that.

Senate hearings on rock lyrics. The size of this medium, the amount of attention it gets, the power people attribute to it, the endless gossip and

opinionizing and information-mongering, it all serves
to wrap a lot of confusion around what is in fact a very
simple form of expression, never very far removed from
the moan of a human voice, the unique keening of a
long high note on an acoustic guitar, the insistent
repetition of the accompanying lower notes, and the
rhythmic thump of a shoe slapping the floor. Robert
Johnson and a thousand like him whose names are lost
to history created or discovered rock and roll, it seems
like discovery because you pick up a guitar and there it
is, like it's always been there, but it feels like creation
because it only happens out of these feelings that won't
not be said and allow no rest until you make a place for
them to express themselves, something different from
the old place...

I'd like to imagine that every adolescent discovers
the meaning of rock and roll the way I did, lying on my
back on a hillside screaming "this could be the last
time!" at the sky. I'd like to think of each and every one
of my rock and roll experiences as being universal, and
once upon a time I could almost believe it, if you
haven't gotten into Buffalo Springfield or the Doors yet
you surely will, it's just a matter of time, old apocalypse
is coming and the voices of the prophets are sounding
and we'll all go together down that slide...

But the monolith shattered, and life went on anyway,
and I didn't die or necessarily grow old but I did grow
up. What now?

Chapter Fifteen

"There's something happening somewhere..."
— Bruce Springsteen

The idiot prepares to hit the road. Bob Dylan's first American tour in five years starts next week, and I plan to fulfill a long-standing promise to myself by attending every one of the first twenty-five or twenty-six concerts of the tour. This will involve six weeks and nine or ten thousand miles of travelling. To justify the time and expense I've had to wangle another book contract, but that's okay, because writing a major book about Dylan's music is another of my long-held dreams. This journey from San Francisco to Houston to Minneapolis to Philadelphia and back, with many stops in between, will mean a lot of solitary hours in my car travelling America's freeways, and so I'm busily converting my records and compact discs into cassette tapes. I'm having fun doing it, and I'm amazed at how many new records I own that I really want to hear a lot more of. It's exciting. Like food on a picnic, rock music always sounds better in an automobile.

There's a game that's played a lot, notably in the letter column of Tower Records' *Pulse* magazine, called DID (Desert Island Discs, which ten records would you choose if you were going to be stranded on a DI along with a phonograph and, I suppose, a bicycle-pedal generator or somesuch?). It's a great game, always fascinating to read people's selections (*Pulse* gets 'em from the readers, which is more fun and more illuminating than critics' choices, and also from the musicians—Jim Kerr of Simple Minds goes for T. Rex's *Get It On*, Lou Reed's *Transformer*, Peter Gabriel's *Biko,* Dylan's *Blood on the Tracks*, David Bowie's *Let's Dance*, U2's *October*, and "anything from" the Doors, Lone Justice, Al Green, and James Brown), satisfying when they name an album you also love, surprising when they name something you're sure couldn't be *any*one's favorite, stimulating when it's a record you haven't heard but could be interested in.

The implication of DIDs is that they're the records you think you'll never get tired of listening to. Young teenagers tend to choose whatever records sound hot to them this week. Then there's people like me who have been putting *Pet Sounds* by the Beach Boys on their DID lists for twenty years—the opposite extreme, my image of what I like to listen to got frozen ages ago and it resists all my efforts to thaw it out.

The funny thing is, I don't listen to *Pet Sounds* (or the Velvet Underground's *Loaded*, or *The Rolling Stones Now,* or *The Byrds' Greatest Hits*, or *Love's Forever Changes*) all the time. A year can easily go by without my listening to any of these records once. But you won't catch me going to a desert island without 'em. That probably has to do with my self-image – we may choose our DIDs based on what we think we want to listen to, but we use them to tell ourselves who we are.

The point I'm getting at, though, is that if instead of the hypothetical desert island I had to choose which ten tapes to take with me this week on a long car trip, my DIDs would be out the window (maybe I'd take one of them, if I hadn't heard it for a while and felt ready to get back into it), because instead of talking about what I imagine I could live with forever, I'd be looking at what do I want to hear right now. (*Candy Apple Grey*, anything by the Violent Femmes and U2, R.E.M.'s *Fables of the Reconstruction*, Feargal Sharkey's album, Prince's *Parade* or one of those early Prince albums I haven't heard yet, maybe *The Hurting* by Tears for Fears and *No Free Lunch* by Green on Red, something by Bob Dylan always, and leave a slot open for whatever I intuitively grab as I walk out the door.)

Both of these people, the one defined by my timeless, desert island rock and roll choices, and the one defined by the rock and roll I feel like listening to today, are real and important parts of me, even though they seem to have little in common. In fact, thinking of it this way clears up something that's been a bit of a mystery to me: why it is I could feel so close to rock and roll, and so out of touch with it, at the same time.

My relationship with rock and roll is both immediate and eternal, and in a real sense it's two different relationships. The eternal one has always been there, perhaps it was there even before I bought my first single (*Charlie Brown* by the Coasters) when I was ten, which is why the music seemed so natural to me when I did connect with it (at age ten, again at sixteen after my folk and blues era, again at thirty-seven and so forth), because the relationship already existed and so when I opened my ears I could just tap right into it, rocking and bopping as if I had always done this, rediscovering the truth. I know I'm not alone in experiencing the sensation that the innermost secrets of my heart have just been broadcast over the radio or discovered in the grooves of an album I spent two weeks' babysitting money for, how did they know? How did they know with such certainty they didn't even have to put it in words, they could communicate the whole thing with a flick of a drumstick and a well-timed hint of defiance or enthusiasm in the singer's voice? They knew because when they laid down that track they were riding on their version of the same eternal relationship with the same indescribable source. They were bopping to the beat of the Mystery, and when I heard it I didn't know what it was but I knew it belonged to me. It had that special ring to it, like coming home.

This eternal something doesn't change, has never changed, is not new and is only called rock and roll because that's its name and this is what it looks like and sounds like in the context of this particular half-century, this place and time. And the flags people wave of What Rock and Roll Means to Me, whether the flag is Led Zeppelin or Little Richard or John Lennon or Duran Duran, are simply their way, our way, of acknowledging the messenger who first or most forcefully brought them the news, and so, underneath that, acknowledging their own unbreakable connection to something that will never die, that is a constant source of support, encouragement, nourishment even when all it is is memories and they never even go near a phonograph or a dance hall any more. It doesn't matter. You can't lose what is always yours.

But the other relationship is an immediate one, and it must be renewed each night, each moment, as your attention drifts and is brought back by a fragment of melody or a burst of showmanship or four incredible notes from a bass guitar. It is entirely possible to be fully aware of and place great value on one's eternal relationship with rock and roll, while experiencing little or no immediate relationship with the stuff. It's also normal to imagine that this is an indication of the unhappy state of present-day rock — most of us deal with most things in the world most of the time as if they and not we held the full power to determine the quality of our mutual relationship. But the good news is that it's in the nature of the immediate that it's always available, all you have to do to make contact with it is reach out to it, history and the past and all those ideas in your head disappear when you're in the present. The bad news is that reaching out once is only good once; when the participation stops the experience stops, and the relationship ceases, until the moment when you reach out again.

I want to share with you some comments from a press conference I attended yesterday, a prelude to tonight's concert in San Francisco, the first of six, celebrating the 25th anniversary of the human rights organization Amnesty International. Present at the press conference were most of the artists who will perform tonight: Sting, Bryan Adams, Joan Baez, Peter Gabriel, Lou Reed, and the four members of U2: Bono, The Edge, Larry Mullen, and Adam Clayton (the Neville Brothers and Jackson Browne will also be part of tonight's show). Jack Healey, executive director of Amnesty International USA, and producer Bill Graham were also on the panel.

Jack Healey described Amnesty — a non-partisan organization committed to the release of prisoners of conscience, persons held because of their political beliefs, in all countries of the world — and this series of concerts, which will raise funds for Amnesty's work but, more importantly, is intended to raise public awareness in the U.S. about human rights and about Amnesty International. Amnesty is a participatory organization — members commit themselves, as groups, to letter-writing campaigns that press for the release of individual prisoners. People attending the concerts will be encouraged to send postcards on behalf of particular prisoners, and to consider becoming Amnesty volunteers themselves. The commitment on the part of the musicians involved, two weeks of travelling together and performing benefit shows, is much greater than the commitment required for previous one-day events like Live Aid (and, not surprisingly, it was much harder to find stars willing and able to participate). And Sting and Bono in particular, the biggest "names" on the tour, have made a special effort to educate and prepare themselves to be effective spokespersons for Amnesty, to use the media's interest in them — TV interviews, etc — as a further opportunity to spread the word.

What follows are edited excerpts from the press conference:

Jack Healey: Amnesty is about the free people worrying about the unfree people, and doing something about it.

Peter Gabriel: I'm doing this because I believe that we can motivate a lot of people, and that governments will respond if we shout loudly enough.

Sting: There's a direct link between musicians or communicators and Amnesty, in that without freedom of expression, we can't do our jobs. And so quite selfishly, it's a way of protecting our positions. I think it's for us as well as the people who are being tortured, because what happens in Guatemala could happen here, quite easily.

Questioner: Activism in popular music seems to come in waves and in trends. What do all of you think is necessary to keep this wave that we're on now going?

Bono: I think there are those who wish the doors that were opened with phenomena like Band Aid and Live Aid would close. Some people have suggested to me, "Can we not just get this over with, this charity business, and get back to rock and roll's redundant behavior, like we had in the Seventies?" And there are those of us anxious to keep the doors open, the spirit that made Live Aid a great day and great phenomenon — we want to keep that spirit, we're actually refusing to go back to sleep. We're keeping our eyes open, because out of those doors came a lot of great music, the music that inspired us to play, John Lennon came through those doors, Bob Dylan came through those doors, Lou Reed came through those doors — a lot of people, a lot of the music that personally excited me came through those doors. And it seemed they were shut for a long time, and music became a kind of very boring soundtrack to a people, and I include myself, that were just walking in their sleep. And it's time to wake up. So we're going to use — I mean rock and roll music is noise, I suppose, but it's positive noise, it's noise that's woken us up, and I hope it'll wake some more up.

Sting: What's essential is that these events be unique, there's no point in just repeating the same event year after year. If musicians and artists are going to be involved in human rights, and all the causes, then each time we do it we have to be creative and innovative, because people get bored. I think it's our responsibility to make them interested and keep them constantly excited by what's happening, and I think we're probably well qualified to do that.

Bill Graham: People ask why rock and rollers continue to do these things. It's the most glaring, most positive image you can have of the power of rock and roll, which is the music of the Twentieth Century; and it's the utilization of this power that makes these events possible.

Joan Baez: My excitement about this particular concert is that my skepticism about "aid, aid, aid" has been proven to be wrong. I thought it would happen, and it would die; it would be a fad, and it would be over. And my feeling is that people are distinguishing themselves, as this panel is doing, by saying they prefer to take one more step. And my hope is, of course, that in the process of this we will continue learning, and people will continue feeling, what it's like to really be involved with the brotherhood, sisterhood of humankind. Then you'll be willing to take a risk and it won't feel like one, it'll just be your daily life.

Bono (adding to Baez's comment): This is the age of realization.

Bono (in response to a question about the usefulness of helping individuals instead of trying to change nations): It's also true that a lot of the people arrested are artists, poets, in their own right, and in a lot of cases they have been arrested for precisely that power to change, or to influence change in, their own countries. I think that's an important thing to remember.

Joan Baez: To know that your hero is willing to listen to this (the bad news about torture and what is being done to people), and find out about it, and deal with it, and confront it, and actually become involved, must be enormously important for the young people of this country.

Bono (after a comment by Sting on how the music is returning to activist subjects after a "dark decade"): I don't think a song has to be specifically political to be powerful. Consider the work of somebody like Marvin Gaye. The great power of his work was that it crossed so many barriers: spiritual, sexual, political. And there's another Irishman who was interested in being here, Van Morrison — one of the reasons it would have been so good to have had him on the bill is, he's never — he's not the sort of man who's going to sing a song like, "Torture is a bad thing, man." But when he sings his love songs, they are so powerful as to get through to the part of you that would care about somebody else less free than you. So I hope there's not a hundred thousand garage bands out there all writing songs with really kind of obvious sloganeering. Because it must be just accepted as part and parcel of our artistic life, that we can come out with a very strong statement, or, you can write about more personal things. For me, it's all protest music, and I don't like that word either, but it's all powerful, it's all political, the politics of love if you like.

Sting: All of these issues actually pervade the whole of your life, the sexuality, your personal life, everything. I agree.

Joan Baez: I also think it needn't be the content of the song but the context in which you put it, which is precisely what goes on here. Obviously we needn't, as Bono says, stand up and sing contrived songs about prison and torture; but the fact that we're here, and the fact that this is taking place, puts our music in a certain context that gives it a different point of view, makes it broader.

Bill Graham: The questioner made the point of all these successes. I think success is a twofold thing — the concert itself is a success and people enjoy themselves and the artists get off and the public parties for the day...but what's the ultimate result, what's the aftereffect of that benefit, what is really done? I can only think of many many years ago, the Children's Nursery in Berkeley, their bus broke down, this alternative school, and they came to the musicians in this town, and the Dead and Santana and Janis got together, on a two-week notice, raised fifteen thousand dollars, bought a bus, painted the bus yellow, and for years we saw this bus running through the hills of Berkeley with children in it. And we could feel and see it.

And that's obviously the whole point with Amnesty. We know for a fact that whatever comes out of this will continue a positive onslaught on the inhumanity of many countries. Too many other benefits, people are not aware of what happens afterwards. What I'm always concerned about, with these benefits, is a revivification of the reality of what these artists do, and that's the thing that lasts for me, whatever the cause is, it's the positive use of power. These artists, sitting at this table today, have the talent and the ability to ask thousands of people to come out and buy tickets, raise money for the particular cause that they believe in. And what should really be asked is, what else do you do besides party? Because if these artists get you to come out there and enjoy the day, and you go back to living your life without being affected beyond having a good time, to some extent that's a failure, and none of us want to see that. So hopefully the ultimate power that these artists have is that the fan will react by relating to Amnesty International, or the farmer, or the homeless; and I can't speak enough for the contribution of the artists at this table, because that is the most positive use of power that I can think of.

Sting: I want to say that, this might sound strange, but I think to be a member of Amnesty International has a certain component of fun in it, in that to have some fascist dictator as a pen pal is a great irony to me. The fact that you can write to this guy, and hopefully try and change his mind, is something that is kind of fun, you know. I think that to be a member of this organization has that component in it, and we shouldn't forget it. It's a very serious and a tragic thing we're talking about, but to belong to it makes you feel good, and I think the people who come to the concert and enjoy the music, we can extend that idea by asking them to become members. Have these people as your pen-pals. Make a nuisance of yourself. Kids like that.

Questioner: Bono, how do you feel about the concert itself, I mean about performing? Are you all going to do some things together, musically are you excited about playing in this context?

Bono: Yeah. I must say that I personally feel a lot more comfortable talking about these issues through the music, than doing it at conference tables, because I'm not really used to this kind of situation. So I'm really looking forward to being on stage, I'll be a lot more relaxed, and I think more effective. I think we're all going to do things together, yes. It is going to be a bit of a party, and I think this is really important, what Sting is saying, like when we come out here we're a little uncomfortable, so we're kind of looking very deep and meaningful, 'cause that's an easy one, but actually backstage is a really good feeling, and there's a lot of laughter. And I hope that comes across. I'm really excited about this.

Lou Reed: Rock and roll to me represents freedom, not only just lyrically, expression of whatever it is you want to write about in a rock and roll song, but the drums and the guitar, that to me has been a political statement, just the energy and the freedom of a rock and roll song. And to me it all relates directly to Amnesty International. If the rebellious side of rock and roll is what appeals to you...

The Edge (following a discussion about finding inner peace versus taking action in the world): Yeah, another point...I think fellow feeling is actually quite a big step in feeling inner peace, as you say; I think it's also the preserving salt of society, its ability to care for other societies or others within its society. When you remember that this country was established on the human rights and civil liberties principles that Amnesty International is actually fighting for for individuals in other countries, I think it's a little sad that there are not more people involved in this great organization in this country. And we want to try and turn people's attention back to the principles on which America was founded, and point these things out again, and say, "Come on, let's remember exactly what this country's all about."

So in a few hours Donna and I leave for what promises to be an evening of human rights education and great rock and roll, at the Cow Palace in San Francisco. (The last show of the tour will be an all-day affair at Giants Stadium in New Jersey; it will be broadcast on national radio and television, and should attract a lot of attention.) I'm excited — excited that I'm going to see U2 perform at last, and excited to be a small part of what feels like a rising tide again.

Bill Graham pointed out during yesterday's press conference that just a few days ago there was a much-publicized, large-scale rock and roll concert in Moscow, a benefit to aid victims of the Chernobyl nuclear accident, the first such charity event in the Soviet Union. The world is changing — barriers truly are being broken down — and rock and roll is playing an important part. Far from being at the end of its tether, rock may be just beginning its greatest era. If this is so, it isn't because of the popularity of the music as such (American television programs are far more popular, here and internationally), but because of its vitality, its aliveness, the commitment it expresses and that its listeners ultimately demand...its ability to tell the truth and wake us from our sleep.

The rock and roll I love is on the one hand a concept, a spirit, a sound (most of all a sound), and a way of being; it is the symbol of the time I live in and grew up in, this set of years in this particular century, which in truth have far more to do with who I am than the nation I live in and grew up in does. And on the other hand the rock and roll I love is something very concrete and actual, even if you can't hit it with a hammer — it's a particular set of records, rhythms, riffs, attitudes, it's tonight's concert and tomorrow's club date, not the concept of those events but the experience itself, me standing near the front of the crowd, stage left, watching and listening to and dancing with and feeling Green on Red at the Berkeley Square or X at Wolfgang's. It's me this afternoon discovering I like the new Stones album a lot more than I thought I did, and as soon as I finish writing this I'm going to tape it for my trip. It's me in the car experiencing indescribable ecstasies (and carefully keeping my foot from pressing down too hard on the accelerator) as I listen to Them singing and playing *Baby Please Don't Go*. It's a set of specifics, details, moments, an open-ended set in which what isn't known is more important and more interesting and exciting than what's already been experienced and identified as wonderful. It's turning on the radio and hoping to hear something new —

In the end, the idiot's an idiot because the map he's staring at is blank. The territory hasn't been explored yet. The possibilities are limitless. Institutions and traditions are powerless here. The real journey starts this evening. The universe is about to be born.

Index